D1422967

The Luftwaffe Fighters' Battle of Britain

Other Chris Goss titles available from Crécy Publishing

The Luftwaffe Bombers' Battle of Britain
The inside story: July-October 1940
Companion volume to *The Luftwaffe Fighters' Battle of Britain*

Bloody Biscay
The story of the Luftwaffe's only long range maritime fighter unit,
V *Gruppe/Kampfgeschwader* 40, and its adversaries 1942-1944

Brothers in Arms
An account of August-September 1940 through the deeds of two opposing
fighter units – 609 Squadron of the RAF and 1/JG53, a Luftwaffe *Staffel*
based in northern France

The Luftwaffe Fighters' Battle of Britain

The inside story: July-October 1940

Chris Goss

Crécy Publishing Limited

Published in 2000 by Crécy Publishing Limited
All rights reserved

© Christopher H. Goss 2000

Christopher H. Goss is hereby identified as the author of this work in accordance with Section 77 of the Copyright, Designs and Patents Act 1988

A CIP record for this book is available from the British Library

ISBN 0 947554 81 5

LEICESTER CITY LIBRARIES	
0947554815	1 694 31
Cypher	13.12.00
940.5449	£19.95

Front cover:
Main: A Messerschmitt BF 110 C of 6/ZG, France, summer 1940
Top: *Oblt* Klaus Quaet-Faslem, Gruppen Adjutant III/JG 53; died in an accident on 30 January 1944 having achieved forty-nine kills and been awarded the *Ritterkreuz*

Printed and bound by Redwood Books, Trowbridge

Crécy Publishing Limited
1a Ringway Trading Estate, Shadowmoss Road, Manchester M22 5LH

Contents

Acknowledgements

I have been writing to, and collecting accounts of, German pilots and their RAF opponents for the last twenty years. It is therefore sad to say that many who have unknowingly helped me and contributed to this book are no longer with us. Therefore, I owe a great debt of thanks to all whose accounts feature in this book and only hope that I have managed to portray their trials and tribulations in a fitting manner.

However, there are a number of friends and acquaintances whose help has been gratefully received:

My good friends Mark Postlethwaite (for the proofreading, constructive criticism and encouragement) and Bernd Rauchbach (for the translating, proofreading and continued help with research). Peter Cornwell, that mine of information on anything 'Battle of Britain', for his assistance with a number of photographs and (Uncle) John Smith for giving me the original idea for this book.

The following all helped in one way or another – they are listed in no particular order:

Wolfgang Falck, the late Air Cdre A. C. Deere, the late *Generalleutnant* Adolf Galland, Mrs Jennifer Dexter, Hans Hoeller, Cato Guhnfeld, Michael Payne, Bill Norman, Eberhard d'Elsa, Ray Stebbings, Geoff Rayner, the late Heinz Dudeck, the late Hans Ohly, the late Willi Morzinek, *Dr* Felix Sauer, Ernst-Albrecht Schulz, Rolf Pingel, Franz Fiby, Walter Rupp, the late Gp Capt Alec Ingle, Ludwig von Eimannsberger, Patrick Burgess, Peter May, *Generalleutnant* Herbert Wehnelt, Herbert Quehl, Josef Volk and Ian Hutton.

Finally, thanks again to my wife Sally and daughters Katherine, Megan and Alexandra – I hope that my hiding in the study all those hours was not too much of an imposition on family life.

Glossary and Abbreviations

AA	Anti-aircraft
Adj	Adjutant
Adler Angriff	Attack of Eagles – 13 August 1940, also known as *Adler Tag* – Eagle Day
Bf	Bayerische Flugzeugwerke (Messerschmitt aircraft prefix used by Germans)
Bordfunker (BF)	Radio operator
De Wilde	Tracer ammunition
Deckungsrotte	Lookout pair
Deflection	Aim off a weapon to allow for its target's velocity
DFC	Distinguished Flying Cross
DFM	Distinguished Flying Medal
Ditch	Force-land in the sea
Do	Dornier
DSO	Distinguished Service Order
Einzelmeldung	Detailed report listing air activities on a daily basis
Erprobungsgruppe	Experimental Wing
Experte	Ace
Feldwebel (Fw)	Flight Sergeant
Fg Off	Flying Officer
Flak	Anti-aircraft fire
Flt Lt	Flight Lieutenant
Flt Sgt	Flight Sergeant
Flt	Flight
Flugzeugfuehrer (F)	Pilot
Freie Jagd	Free hunting fighter sweep
Fuehrer	Leader
Gefreiter (Gefr)	Leading Aircraftman
Generalfeldmarschall	Air Chief Marshal
Geschwader (Gesch)	Group consisting of three *Gruppen*; commanded by a *Geschwader Kommodore (Gesch Komm)*
Gp Capt	Group Captain

Gp	Group
Gruppe (Gr)	Wing consisting of three *Staffeln*; commanded by a *Gruppen Kommandeur (Gr Kdr)*. *Gruppe* number denoted by Roman numerals (eg. II)
Hauptmann (Hptm)	Flight Lieutenant
He	Heinkel
Holzauge	Lookout
Ia	Operations Officer
Inj	Injured
Jabo	Fighter-bomber
Jafue	Fighter Leader or operational level of command
Jagdgeschwader (JG)	Fighter Group
Ju	Junkers
Kamerad	Friend
Kampfgeschwader (KG)	Bomber Group
Kampfgruppe	Bomber group or formation
Katchmarek	Wingman
Kette	Three aircraft tactical formation similar to a vic
Kph	Kilometres per hour
Lehrgeschwader (LG)	Technical Development Flying Group
Leutnant (Lt)	Pilot Officer
Luftflotte	Air Fleet
Major (Maj)	Squadron Leader
Me	Messerschmitt (used by RAF)
Nachrichtenoffizier (NO)	Communications Officer
Oberfeldwebel (Ofw)	Warrant Officer (WO)
Obergefreiter (Ogefr)	Senior Aircraftman
Oberleutnant (Oblt)	Flying Officer
Oberst	Group Captain
Oberstleutnant (Obstlt)	Wing Commander
Plt Off	Pilot Officer
POW	Prisoner of War
Reichsmarschall	Marshal of the Air Force
Revi	Reflector gunsight
Rotte	Two aircraft tactical formation; two *Rotten* made a *Schwarm*; commanded by a *Rottenfuehrer*
Rottenflieger	Wingman

RPM	Revolutions per minute
Schwarm	Four aircraft tactical formation; commanded by a *Schwarm Fuehrer*
Seeloewe	Sealion – German code name for the invasion of Great Britain
Seenotflugkommando	Air Sea Rescue Detachment
Sonderstaffel	Special *Staffel*
Sqn Ldr	Squadron Leader
Sqn	Squadron
Stab	Staff or Headquarters; formation in which *Gr Kdr* and *Gesch Komm* flew
Stabsfeldwebel (Stfw)	Senior Warrant Officer
Staffel (St)	Squadron (twelve aircraft); commanded by a *Staffel Kapitaen (St Kap)*. *Staffel* number denoted by Arabic numerals (eg. 2)
Stuka	Junkers 87
Sturzkampfgeschwader (StG)	Dive Bomber Group
Technischer Offizier (TO)	Technical Officer
Uninj	Uninjured
Unteroffizier (Uffz)	Sergeant (Sgt)
Vic	Three aircraft tactical formation used by the RAF
W	Wounded
Werk Nummer (Wk Nr)	Serial number
Wg Cdr	Wing Commander
Zerstoerer (Z)	Destroyer
Zerstoerergeschwader (ZG)	Heavy fighter group
+	Killed

Introduction

Like many others, I have always been fascinated by stories of the Battle of Britain and how the outnumbered RAF fought and defeated a far superior enemy, namely the fighter and bomber aircraft of the *Luftwaffe*. For obvious reasons, accounts of what happened during the summer of 1940 tended to be centred around the defenders, be they in the air or on the ground. However, what started to interest me was the story of the Battle of Britain from the other side. That story went largely untold – a fate always meted out to those who are on the losing side or team.

Twenty years ago, I started contacting those German aircrew who participated in the Battle of Britain, most of whom had been taken prisoners of war. At the same time, I attempted to trace where their aircraft crashed, who was responsible for their demise and, in some cases, put the victor and the vanquished in contact with each other. Over the years, a series of very personal, sometimes harrowing, sometimes heroic, sometimes tragic, stories have emerged which, when put in chronological order, give an interesting insight into the Battle of Britain from the antagonist's point of view. One must never lose sight of the fact that the *Luftwaffe* was an instrument of Adolf Hitler's evil designs for the world but, despite this, inside the German fighter and bomber aircraft were very ordinary people who had the misfortune to be born at the wrong time.

The Luftwaffe Fighters' Battle of Britain and its accompanying volume *The Luftwaffe Bombers' Battle of Britain* are the result of some twenty years of research which will hopefully allow the reader to see the Battle of Britain from a different perspective. The books are by no means comprehensive and definitive stories of the Battle of Britain but they will allow the reader to understand how it felt to be flying against a tenacious enemy who had nothing to lose and how it felt to be defeated when, for the previous year, all that the *Luftwaffe* had faced was, in the main, a combination of disorganised, technically and numerically inferior opponents.

Prologue to the Battle

The fighter pilots of the *Luftwaffe* had experienced a relatively quiet war prior to spring 1940. During the invasion of Poland, they met a very tenacious opponent flying aircraft that were far inferior to their Messerschmitt 109s and 110s. Again, during the invasion of Scandinavia, their opponents were equally tenacious but were numerically inferior. The invasion of the Low Countries saw them pitted against a series of enemies who adopted different tactics to counter the German technical and numerical superiority and had to change and adapt these tactics whilst constantly retreating. Just eighteen days after the Germans launched their offensive in the west, Belgium capitulated and German forces were poised to crush the remnants of the British Expeditionary Force and their allies along the north-eastern coast of France. Meanwhile in Norway, British forces in the Narvik region, together with French and Polish troops, having recaptured the town from the German invasion force, were fighting a desperate rearguard action against a superior German force in that area.

Two *Luftwaffe* fighter pilots were about to experience first hand what the rest of the *Luftwaffe* would experience in the months to come. *Oblt* Hans Jaeger of 3/ZG 76 had scored his *Gruppe*'s second kill of the war when, on 2 September 1939, he had shot down a Polish PZL 24. In April 1940, prior to the German invasion of Norway, he had been moved to become the *Gruppen Adjutant* of I/ZG 76. However, on 11 May 1940, he was ordered to form a *Sonderstaffel* from the more experienced pilots within the *Gruppe,* its task being to provide fighter support for the Luftwaffe's bombers still attacking British forces in the Narvik area. To maximise their range and to increase the time on patrol, the Messerschmitt 110 D-1/R-1 was used, a sub-variant which used the 1,050 litre fuel tank known as the 'Dachshund belly' by its crews.

Flying from Trondheim, the *Staffel* commenced its first flight on 20 May 1940, the same day that the RAF re-established

Oblt *Hans Jaeger (right) with* Lt *Heinz Holborn (left) and* Hptm *Reinecke (centre),* Gr Kdr *of I/ZG 76.* (Kettling)

A long range tank being fitted to Ofw Gerhard Herzog's Bf 110D-1 of 1/ZG 76.
(Kettling)

itself in northern Norway. Seven days later, on the first day that Allied troop reinforcements landed at Narvik, a *Schwarm* which was headed by Hans Jaeger escorting *Stukas* attacking Bodo, met RAF fighters for the first time:

Flight Lieutenant Caesar Hull, 263 Squadron

Got the Gladiator going and shot off without helmet or waiting to do anything up. Circled the 'drome, climbing, and pinned an '87 at the bottom of its dive. It made off slowly over the sea and just as I was turning away, another '87 shot past me and shots went through my windscreen, knocking me out for a while. Came to and was thanking my lucky stars when I heard a rat-tat behind me and I felt my Gladiator hit. Went into a right-hand turn and dive but could not get out of it. Had given up hope at 200ft when she centralised and I gave her a burst of engine to clear some large rocks. Further rat-tats behind me so gave up hope and decided to get down. Held off, then crashed.

Hull had fallen victim to Jaeger's *Rottenflieger*, Lt Helmut Lent, whilst Jaeger claimed to have shot down another, believed to have been Lt Tony Lydekker RN who was wounded; it was his fourth and last kill. If the German crews thought that future meetings with RAF fighters would be this easy, they were soon to be proved wrong as they found out two days later when the whole *Staffel* flew to Bardufoss on an escort sortie:

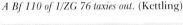

A Bf 110 of 1/ZG 76 taxies out. (Kettling)

Oberleutnant Hans Jaeger, I/ZG 76

On this sortie, *Hptm* Werner Restemeyer, our *Gruppen Kommandeur*, led the formation of eight aircraft; I flew as his *Rottenflieger*. We were attacked, to my great surprise, at an altitude of 5,000m by Hurricanes coming from above. I received several hits in both engines which were damaged and I had to dive away. I was forced to land in the sea 100m off the coast at Salanger. My *Bordfunker*, *Uffz* Helmut Feick, and I were not wounded but we were captured by Polish soldiers soon after we had swum to shore. The next day we were brought to Harstad and a few days later to London.

Hans Jaeger had never before encountered a 'modern' RAF fighter, 46 Squadron having landed at Bardufoss just two days before. In addition to Hans Jaeger being shot down, *Hauptmann* Restemeyer's fighter was badly hit and his *Bordfunker* badly wounded. They were probably victims of either Sgt Stanley Andrew, Flt Sgt Edward Shackley or Fg Off Phillip Frost.

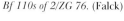

Bf 110s of 2/ZG 76. (Falck)

As Hans Jaeger was being marched away to captivity, over the beaches of north-eastern France, the *Luftwaffe* was now facing an RAF which was operating from established homeland bases and for the first time, its full arsenal of fighters – Spitfires, Hurricanes and Defiants – were being used. Just after dawn on 1 June 1940, a formation of about forty-eight Spitfires were patrolling the Belgian/French coast. For one German pilot, it was to be his first and last meeting with Spitfires:

Oberleutnant **Juergen Moeller,** *Staffelfuehrer* **2/ZG 1**

My *Staffel Kapitaen*, *Oblt* Horst Lehrmann, was not flying this day and I was leading the *Staffel*. I was at the head of about twelve aircraft and we were flying over Dunkirk when we encountered some Spitfires. They flew directly opposite to our course. We had been told that it would be very unlikely that we would be involved in a frontal attack but if we ever were, we should never change course – whoever turns first or loses his nerve would die. So when I saw the Spitfires, I did exactly that, hoping that the RAF pilot would lose his nerve first. Either he was as stubborn as me or, this seems a strong possibility in retrospect, he was already dead. Witnesses noted that he did not fire in the last seconds. Both of us did not give an inch. He crashed into my right wing and tore it off. His 'plane exploded because I hit the centre of his aircraft. Both my *Bordfunker*, *Uffz* Karl Schieferstein, and myself parachuted to safety, landing amongst the thousands of soldiers on the beach.

Oblt *Juergen Moeller*. (Moeller)

Three Messerschmitt 110s of I/ZG 1 were shot down in this combat but, despite the superiority in numbers, it is believed that at least two Spitfires from 41 Squadron and four from 222 Squadron were lost when Messerschmitt 109s intervened. The aircraft that brought down *Oblt* Moeller is thought to have been flown either by Fg Off Gerald Massey-Sharpe or Sgt Leslie White of 222 Squadron, neither of whom survived. Nevertheless, it gave the RAF confidence when attacking the so-called Messerschmitt 110 'destroyer', despite the German belief that they would win any head on attack, as the following combat report, filed on 1 June 1940, shows:

Pilot Officer Timothy Vigors, 222 Squadron

A formation of twelve Me 110s were seen diving through the clouds. 19 Squadron attacked, driving a few back into the clouds. An Me 110 appeared through the cloud, 150 yards ahead and above me coming directly towards me. I opened fire at 100 yards and saw the enemy fly straight into my fire. One of the crew escaped by parachute...

By 4 June 1940, a total of 316,663 troops had been evacuated as part of Operation Dynamo; ten days later the Germans entered Paris. The French sued for peace on 22 June 1940, shortly after the final RAF elements withdrew to Great Britain. It was then left to the British Prime Minister and German *Fuehrer* to give an indication of what was to follow:

Winston Churchill

What General Weygand called the Battle of France is over. I expect that the Battle of Britain is about to begin. The whole fury and might of the enemy must very soon be turned on us. Hitler knows that he will have to break us in this island or lose the war...

Adolf Hitler

As England, despite her hopeless military situation, still shows no sign of willingness to come to terms, I have decided to and if necessary to carry out a landing operation against her... The aim of this operation is to eliminate the English motherland as a base from which war against Germany can be continued and if necessary, to occupy the Country completely.

In order to realise Hitler's aim, the *Luftwaffe* had firstly to achieve and maintain air superiority over the English Channel. They had not experienced the Channel during any previous invasions of the war. Their

A Bf 110C of I/ZG 1. (via Diener)

single seat fighters would be operating at maximum range. They had already seen shortfalls in the effectiveness of their twin-engined fighters and this time they would be facing an enemy with far superior fighters, operating from their own bases, over their own territory and possessing an effective early warning system. If the German aircrews thought that this time they might find things harder, they were soon to find out.

1
The Battle Begins – July 1940

July 1940 started quietly for the German fighter pilots who must have been keen for a rest after their efforts during the previous two months. Initially, the *Luftwaffe* restricted its efforts to a series of reconnaissance flights and probing attacks on coastal targets along the length and breadth of Britain. The first co-ordinated major attack, with fighter escort, did not occur until the 4th of the month. From then on the tempo began to increase.

As well as escort flights, the German fighters enjoyed what were called *Freie Jagd*, literally free chases or fighter sweeps. Such missions soon inflicted a heavy price on unsuspecting RAF fighters over the Channel. However, the German fighter pilots soon began to dislike the regular flights escorting the much slower bomber and reconnaissance aircraft. For *Lt* Albert Striberny of 3/LG 2, such a mission would prove to be his downfall; he was destined to become the last German casualty before what would become officially known as the first day of the Battle of Britain:

Leutnant **Albert Striberny, 3/LG 2**

8 July – we were just about to leave the airfield at Ste Inglevert. It was rather late, about 2030 hrs, and we had our lodgings in Wissant, a little bathing resort between Cap Gris-Nez and Calais. Just then, a Dornier 17 landed on the airfield, the telephone rang and I was ordered to see our *Geschwader Kommodore*. I found him with a *Major* and his crew from the Do 17; he had to undertake a reconnaissance flight over Dover and the surroundings and my *Staffel* was ordered to escort them.

Not being very pleased after a long day's business and as it was evening, we agreed that we would fly at 4,500m altitude. Our *Staffel* had only five aircraft available for the task (normally twelve) so we started in a three and two aircraft formation, the latter *Rotte* to protect us. Having reached an altitude of 4,500m over the Channel we found ourselves in sunshine but saw that there were a lot of cumulus clouds over the English coast and Dover. The Do 17, contrary to our agreement, dived into the clouds and us three Bf 109s had to move together and follow him.

The remains of Striberny's Bf 109. (via Cornwell)

At about 1,700m, the clouds ended and together we flew over Dover. Besides photographing, the Dornier threw out some small bombs and then climbed back into cloud and we again joined up and followed. When the clouds ended, I quickly noticed the Do 17 near us but then, much higher, saw the sun shining on many aircraft – Spitfires!

Our situation was bad – low speed due to climbing through the cloud and so many aircraft coming down on us with the advantage of speed. I think now of the clear silhouette of our three aircraft against the white clouds.

In spite of our efforts to try and gain more speed, in no time they were on us and the battle was short. Whilst I was behind a Spitfire, another was behind me. I heard the sound as if one throws peas against a metal sheet and my cabin was full of dark smoke. I felt splashes of fuel on my face so I switched off the electrical system, dived back into cloud and threw off the cabin roof. The smoke disappeared and I could breathe freely and noticed that from the wings there came white streams of glycol. Whilst diving, I tried several times to start the engine, switching on the electrical system, but in vain. When I came out of cloud, I decided to bale out and undid the clasp of my seat belt and was about to climb onto the seat and jump when I thought of the high speed of the aircraft and I was afraid to be thrown against the tailplane so I pulled back the stick and slowed the aircraft down. This took a matter of seconds; I did a half roll and fell out.

As I was a bit afraid to mix up the handle for opening the parachute and the press-button that holds the parachute straps, I put my right hand on the handle and rolled the aircraft with the left. When falling, I didn't notice very much but, as we were told, counted to twenty-three then pulled the handle and after the drogue had opened over me, I felt a sudden jerk and hung under the opened parachute. There was no noise and I felt fixed to the sky. Then came the aircraft that shot me down – circling round me very close so I made a gesture with my hand that he should go away which he did and I was alone.

The wind from the west swept the parachute and me in a swinging motion and I drew with my weight and hands the lines of it to stop this movement as I didn't want to land in the sea. I had, of course, a life jacket but thought it better to land on a dry place.

By and by, but very slowly, I came nearer the earth. Below me on a road I noticed a bus and an ambulance. In the pocket of my trousers, I had an old silver pocket watch of my grandfather's. I took it out and opened the case and remember it was about 2130 hrs The feeling of falling down got stronger and when the horizon came up, I landed very softly in a gully in swampy land with a layer of moss. With a push, I freed myself from my parachute and waited for what was to come.

Albert Striberny had fallen victim to a patrolling Spitfire from 54 Squadron whose pilot filed a very comprehensive and conclusive report:

Flight Lieutenant Basil Way, 'B' Flight Commander, 54 Squadron

I was leading three sections of the Squadron with orders to patrol Dover at 3,000ft. Whilst orbiting over the coast, I was informed by RT that there were three Me 109s at 12,000ft in the vicinity. I was at 5,000ft and proceeded to climb. I saw two aircraft behind Green Section – I warned them that they might be enemy and former [sic] turned towards cloud. I continued to climb and immediately aircraft began to execute climbing spiral turns. I got right behind them (identified as Me 109s) – they were in vic formation and I attacked rear one, giving it a three second burst from astern at 200 yards. I don't think that enemy aircraft

'A' Flt 54 Sqn just before Dunkirk. Basil Way is sitting 2nd from the right. (Deere)

could have seen me until the moment of the attack. Glycol began to pour from its radiator with a certain amount of black smoke. I left this enemy aircraft and turned to attack the second. The second enemy aircraft dived straight down and I managed to get a long burst at 250 yards. Enemy aircraft continued to dive, skirting edge of cloud, 9,000ft

Another 8 July 1940 victim – Lt Johann Boehm of 4/JG 51 was shot down by 74 Sqn.

The pilot that shot him down was Sgt Tony Mould. (May)

over the coast. It came below and at 5,000ft, pilot baled out. I judged his position as five miles inland, north-west of Deal; parachute opened.

Sadly, Basil Way did not last the month. Shot down and killed off Dover on 25 July, his body was later washed ashore in France and buried near Dunkirk.

As the tempo increased, additional fighter *Geschwader* were moved from rest in Germany to bases all along France's northern coast. Further to the west, as targets were further away from France and as the range of the single seat fighters was limited, escorting the bombers was left in the main to Messerschmitt 110s. One of the first combats with these twin-engined fighters took place on 9 July when III/ZG 26 learned a painful lesson when they lost three aircraft to the Hurricanes of 56 Squadron with a further Messerschmitt limping home badly damaged. It would appear that the pain of the losses was tempered by what they claimed to have shot down – five Hurricanes and seven Spitfires. In fact, none were lost to German fighters.

Just as one Messerschmitt 110 unit suffered at the hands of the RAF, another, this time further west, was to undergo a similar fate. *Oblt* Gerhard Kadow, *Staffel Kapitaen* of 9/ZG 76, had already had an eventful war to date. On 8 June 1940, he and three other crews from the Messerschmitt 110

Oblt Gerhard *Kadow (front centre) seen as a POW in Canada, Summer 1944. (Kadow)*

equipped II/ZG 1 (which was later reformed as III/ZG 76) had been shot down by Swiss Messerschmitt 109s near Morteau. This had occurred because the Swiss Air Force had taken a tough stance against the frequent border incursions by German aircraft. Following a number of air battles, on 8 June the *Luftwaffe* attempted to provoke Swiss fighters into battle and then to inflict heavy losses on them. In fact the opposite occurred and this pointless tactic cost the lives of three men, one of whom was Gerhard Kadow's *Bordfunker*; Kadow himself was wounded.

With the Battle of France over, Gerhard Kadow's unit based itself at Laval in France where, recovered from his wounds, he was teamed up with a new *Bordfunker*, *Gefr* Helmut Scholz. On 11 July, it was his destiny to be shot down again:

Oberleutnant **Gerhard Kadow**, *Staffel Kapitaen* **9/ZG 76**

On 11 July 1940, we flew from Laval to Dinard to refuel and then towards England at 1200 hrs. My *Staffel* together with the other two from the *Gruppe* were ordered to protect *Stukas* which had targets in the Portland area.

Kadow's Bf 110. (via Cornwell)

Just before we took off, my *Geschwader Kommodore*, *Maj* Walter Grabmann, briefed us that it was imperative that no *Stuka* could be lost, even if it meant the loss of our fighters. On that day, my *Staffel* had only seven aircraft combat ready and I was briefed to protect the right flank at 4,000m altitude; the other two *Staffeln* had to protect the left flank at 6,000m altitude and provide close escort for the *Stukas* after they had dropped their bombs (the time at which *Stukas* were most vulnerable).

For much of the flight across the Channel, it was uneventful but as we approached the British coast, we were confronted by the enemy. I counted about twenty dark specks in the distance, somewhat higher than we were and when they came nearer, I was certain that they were British fighters but could not say whether they were Spitfires or Hurricanes.

I knew that my twin-engined fighter was not as manoeuvrable as a single-seat fighter so the chances of winning were reduced. The proportion of British fighters to my *Staffel* was about 3:1 but I had to follow our orders of protecting the *Stukas*. Relying on my two cannon and four forward facing guns, I carried out a head-on attack on the first fighter – I pressed all buttons and the bullets flew out like water out of a watering can. Our closing speed was very fast and both of us broke away in order not to collide. Whether I had any success I do not know, as in the next instant two other British fighters were behind me and opened fire. My engines stopped and I knew that getting home was impossible. My enemy saw his success and stopped shooting but followed me. I threw off the cabin roof (in the hope that it might hit one of the attacking fighters!) and I ordered Scholz to do the same. However, he reported that the mechanism to do this had been damaged by gunfire so because of this, I decided not to bale out or ditch in the Channel.

Because of all the above, I decided to make a crash-landing which I did so with success on Povington Heath near Wareham in Dorset at about 1245 hrs. After the crash-landing, I could not leave the aircraft immediately as a bullet had hit my seat and the damage that it had caused meant that the rough edges of the aluminium had snagged my parachute and flying suit. However, I managed to get out and helped out my *Bordfunker* who had suffered slight wounds from bullet splinters.

The first thing I decided to do was to destroy the aircraft. At this time we did not have an explosive charge to do this, so we opened the fuel tanks and then I tried to set the fuel on fire with my pistol. I used up eight bullets but without success. As this was going on, I heard impacts probably from bullets. I went to the other side of the aircraft to find out and immediately felt a blow to my heel – a bullet had entered the sole of my flying boot just as I was taking a step. The heel helped deflect the bullet which caused just a slight flesh wound. After this, we both left the aircraft alone and looked around us.

About twenty soldiers stood up and an officer ordered us to put our hands up – we did just that and became prisoners of war. I complained that it was unfair to shoot us fliers who had been shot down. He said that we had been trying to destroy our aircraft and he had tried to prevent us doing just that – be glad, he said, that we had not received a bullet in the belly!

During the air battle, two other aircraft from my *Staffel* had been shot down. One, piloted by *Oblt* Jochen Schroeder, had ditched and both he and his *Bordfunker* had got out. However, the *Bordfunker* had been badly wounded and soon died; Jochen was rescued by a boat. The other Messerschmitt was flown by *Oblt* Hans-Joachim Goering, nephew of *Generalfeldmarschall* Hermann Goering; he was probably mortally wounded and crashed still in the cockpit of his aircraft.

A further Messerschmitt 110 from 7/ZG 76 was lost to a tenacious RAF defence as well as just one of the *Stukas*. Gerhard Kadow's Messerschmitt was claimed by at least five RAF pilots from different squadrons. It is believed that the head-on attack that he reported was against Hurricanes of 238 Squadron but the credit for his demise went to another two pilots:

Sqn Ldr John Dewar.

Squadron Leader John Dewar, 87 Squadron

Having disposed of one Me 110, I went into a full turn to review the progress of the battle and to remove two other enemy aircraft trying to get onto my tail. I saw a bomb explode by some shipping in the harbour and two enemy aircraft diving for the ground. One enemy aircraft was still pursuing me. The Hurricane turned easily onto his tail – he was vertically banked. He then dived for ground going east. I followed but withheld fire as I was getting short of rounds. Enemy aircraft pulled out at about 1,000ft and continued 'S' turns. I gave him a burst from 100 yards and vapour came from both engines. I had to slam the throttle back to avoid overshooting. Vapour then ceased to come from the engines and he gathered way again. I was very close and saw no rear gun fire so I held my position and took careful non-deflection shots, using all ammunition. Enemy aircraft at once turned inland, going very slowly. Seeing me draw away, he turned seawards again. I went to head him off and he, apparently thinking I had more rounds, turned for land again, sinking slowly. At 200ft, another Hurricane came up and fired a short burst at him [Fg Off H K Riddle of 601 Sqn]. He immediately turned and landed on Grange Heath. Both crew got out wearing yellow life jackets. The Army were close by…

The scene was setting for the *Luftwaffe* for the remainder of the Battle of Britain but for the rest of the month of July 1940 fighter combats remained sporadic with no side emerging as the clear winner. For example, on 19 July the twin seat Boulton Paul Defiants of 141 Squadron were bounced by *Hptm* Hannes Trautloft's III/JG 51. Trautloft and the three other members of his *Stabschwarm*, *Oblt* Otto Kath, *Lt* Werner Pichon-Kalau and *Lt* Herbert

The victorious Stab III/JG 51, St Omer/Clairmarais, Summer 1940. *Left to Right* Oblt Otto Kath *(Adj)*, Lt Werner Pichon-Kalau *(TO)*, Lt Herbert Wehnelt *(NO)*, Hptm Hannes Trautloft *(Gr Kdr)*. (Wehnelt)

Wehnelt, led the attack which resulted in the destruction of six Defiants and damaged a further one; in human terms, four pilots and six gunners were killed with a further three pilots wounded. The Squadron was immediately withdrawn from the battle. For the *Luftwaffe*, the worst day for fighter losses was 24 July when JG 26 lost four aircraft. Of the four pilots, three were killed and one taken prisoner and of those, one pilot was a *Gruppen Kommandeur*, another the *Gruppe Technischer Offizier*. JG 52 fared no better, also losing four aircraft of which all four pilots were killed. Again, of those four, one was a *Gruppen Kommandeur* and two were *Staffel Kapitaene*. The losses of three *Gruppe* executives necessitated III/JG 52 being withdrawn from France. On this day, for one German pilot, this was his first combat over England. *Hptm* Adolf Galland was leading III/JG 26 and recalls clearly what happened:

Hauptmann **Adolf Galland,** *Gruppen Kommandeur* **III/JG 26**

On 24 July, I obtained my fifteenth victory. It was at about 1335 hrs, thirty kilometres north of Margate at an altitude of 2,200–3,000m. I could see the enemy pilot at the time he jumped out of his aircraft but unfortunately his parachute did not open. I did notice that the Spitfire crashed onto the water.

There was only one pilot fatality in this combat. Plt Off Johnny Allen of 54 Squadron was killed when his Spitfire crashed into an electricity sub-station at Margate. Galland's victim cannot be identified for sure on a day that reinforced Galland's belief that the RAF would be a difficult and tenacious opponent. During the same action, thirty year-old *Oblt* Lothar Ehrlich, *Staffel Kapitaen* of 8/JG 52 was seen by his comrades to have baled out in the middle of the Channel in between Dover and Calais following combat with a Spitfire. The victorious RAF pilot also noted the same:

Adolf Galland. (Galland)

Pilot Officer Colin Gray, 54 Squadron

I shot down an Me 109 some time after midday on 24 July 1940 and the pilot baled out into the sea. I saw him swimming for some object which I thought may have been a dinghy and passed details of his location to control but apparently he was not picked up. Whether or not this was *Oblt* Ehrlich, I do not know – the actual location as I remember was eight miles off Margate. If this was Ehrlich, I do not know how anyone else would know the location since I did not see any other aircraft in the vicinity. Nevertheless, it was the enemy aircraft I was after, not the pilot. In fact I was always pleased to see the pilot bale out and, in this case, I did my best to see that he was rescued although, unfortunately, to no avail.

Still the *Luftwaffe* tried to bomb shipping all along the Channel and as the end of the month approached, the weight and fury of their attacks increased. Nevertheless, the RAF managed to weather the storm, not realising that the storm to come would be even stronger. On the 29th of the month, it was decided that the daylight passage of ships through the Dover Straits would only occur during the hours of darkness. However, the day before that a combat took place which could have been an even greater blow to the *Luftwaffe* than the fighter losses that occurred on 24 July:

Oblt *Lothar Ehrlich, 8/JG 52, killed in action 24 July 1940.* (via Quehl)

Major **Werner Moelders,** *Geschwader Kommodore* **JG 51**

I flew on 28 July 1940 with my *Rottenflieger* and *Adjutant*, *Oblt* Erich Kircheis north of Dover. Suddenly I saw three British fighters, far behind them a lot of Spitfires in the haze. The three Spitfires were somewhat below us so I attacked this section. When I approached, both the outer Spitfires turned but the one in the middle flew straight on. I got behind it and opened fire from sixty metres. At once the wing caught fire, thick smoke and flame, and the Spitfire went down. I pulled up and saw eight to ten Spitfires behind me. I was frightened for a moment. There was only one chance – to go straight through the formation. I swept through the crowd. The first Spitfires were surprised but one of the rearmost was watchful. He fired with all guns and hit me! It rattled my aircraft, I had hits in the cooling system, wing and fuel tank. I broke away and dived with everything I had – 700kph towards the Channel. The engine was working well thank God! The Spitfires chased me and my flag of smoke but then *Oblt* Richard Leppla, who had seen the incident, rushed to my assistance. He shot at the Spitfire sitting behind me and, after a few seconds, it went down wrapped in a large cloud of smoke. When I reached the coast, the engine began to splutter and, during the crash-landing, the undercarriage collapsed and I made a perfect belly landing. When I tried to get out, my legs were strangely weak and I saw bloodstains. In hospital I discovered the reason why – three splinters in the thigh, one in the knee and one in the left foot; I had felt nothing in the heat of combat.

Moelders' initial attack wounded Fg Off Tony Lovell of 41 Squadron who managed to nurse his crippled Spitfire back to RAF Manston. It is believed

Maj *Werner Moelders*. (via Moelders)

A Spitfire of 41 Sqn.

that Flt Lt John Webster, also of 41 Squadron, was the pilot who managed to put a quick burst of fire into Moelders' fighter. As the German pilot tried to flee back to France, it was Plt Off Peter Stevenson who tried to finish him off only to be shot down by *Oblt* Leppla.

Despite poor weather conditions, attacks by German bombers continued on the last three days of the month but no German fighters were lost. However, they still managed to inflict losses on the RAF, one casualty being the pilot who wounded Werner Moelders, Flt Lt John Webster, who was hit in combat on 28 July but managed to return to RAF Manston with a damaged Spitfire. Activity on 31 July was severely curtailed by the weather, even if II/JG 51 managed to teach the RAF a final lesson by mauling 74 Squadron who lost two Spitfires and their pilots. The first month of the Battle of Britain then ended. The RAF had realised the effectiveness of the single-seat German fighters but had also realised the failings of the Messerschmitt 110. To the irritation of the German fighter pilots, they had increasingly been called upon to 'wet nurse' bomber and reconnaissance aircraft but when allowed to carry out *Freie Jagd*, could punish the RAF severely. Nevertheless, lessons had been learned on both sides and as July moved into August, both air forces were keen to put these lessons to good advantage.

2
The Pace Quickens – August 1940

With air operations during July 1940 hampered in the main by poor weather, the same can be said of the first week of August 1940. Mist, low cloud and haze seemed to be the pattern for at least the first five days. When, on the 5th of the month, the first fighter combats occurred, neither side emerged the clear winner. However, one of the German injured, *Oblt* Reinhard Seiler, *Staffel Kapitaen* of 1/JG 54 was another casualty that the *Luftwaffe* could do without. A veteran of the Spanish Civil War where he had already claimed nine air combat victories and the Battle of France where he scored a further two, he was wounded in a combat with RAF fighters which meant he was off flying for the remainder of 1940[1].

Three days later, things took a dramatic turn for the worse for the RAF. Regarded by some as the first true day of the Battle of Britain, 8 August 1940 saw the might of the *Luftwaffe* thrown against Convoy CW9, codename PEEWIT. Sailing from Southend in the late afternoon of 7 August, it passed through the Straits of Dover during the hours of darkness, apparently undetected. However, this was not the case for, as dawn started to break the next day, the convoy was attacked by German *E*-boats which scattered the convoy. As the ships approached the Isle of Wight, it was the turn of *Stukas* to finish what the *E*-boats had started.

Despite a heavy fighter escort, the first air attack of the day was successfully parried by Hurricanes of 145 Squadron even if they did lose three aircraft to I and III/JG 27. At lunchtime, with an even bigger escort of both Messerschmitt 109s and 110s, the *Stukas* returned. This time, more RAF fighters were thrown into battle. Plt Off David Crook of 609 Squadron noted in his book *Spitfire Pilot* that there was going to be a lot of trouble that day because the convoy was such a tempting target. His squadron had missed the earlier attack but as the convoy sailed further west and into their 'patch', it was not long before they were in action:

Pilot Officer David Crook, 609 Squadron

We steered towards the convoy which was now about twelve miles

[1]*Oblt* Seiler would end the War having flown over 500 sorties and shot down 109 aircraft. He would also be awarded the Knight's Cross with Oakleaves.

Plt Off David Crook (centre with mug of tea).

south of Bournemouth. There was a small layer of cloud and while dodging in and out of this, Flt Lt McArthur and I got separated from the other three and a moment later, we also lost each other.

While looking around to try and find them, I glanced out towards the convoy and saw three balloons falling in flames. Obviously an attack was starting and I climbed above the cloud layer and went towards the convoy at full throttle, climbing all the time towards the sun so that I could deliver my attack with the sun behind me.

I was now about five miles from the convoy and could see a big number of enemy fighters circling above, looking exactly like a swarm of flies buzzing round a pot of jam. Below them, the dive-bombers were diving down on the ships and great fountains of white foam were springing up where their bombs had struck the water. I could see that one or two ships had already been hit and were on fire.

I was now at 16,000ft above the whole battle and turned round to look for a victim. At that moment, a Hurricane squadron appeared on the scene and attacked right into the middle of the enemy fighters which were split up immediately and a whole series of individual combats started covering a very big area of the sky...

Again, the battle above the convoy raged but the RAF fighters were not able to prevent damage being inflicted on the ships. German fighter kills were filed by I and III/JG 27 who claimed six RAF fighters and the Messerschmitt 110s of V(Z)/LG 1 which claimed a further eleven. These units also claimed eight barrage balloons, the same ones seen by David Crook going down in flames. As if this was not enough, a few hours later the Germans launched a

A Spitfire of 609 Sqn. (Dexter)

further attack against the luckless convoy, the German fighters and bombers again being attacked tenaciously by RAF fighters. This final attack at about tea-time resulted in further claims for II and III/JG 27 and I/ZG 2 but this was to be the last assault on what was left of PEEWIT. Only four ships arrived unscathed at Swanage later than evening – seven had been sunk and another thirteen damaged. The RAF claimed to have shot down thirty-three German aircraft whilst the Germans claimed forty-seven. Actual losses were fourteen RAF fighters and twelve of their pilots killed whilst the *Luftwaffe* lost nine fighters and seven fighter aircrew killed in addition to eight *Stukas*. Although bloodied, the RAF had held its own against superior numbers of German fighters and had gained vital combat experience; the month, and for that matter the Battle of Britain, had only just started.

The following two days were quiet with little action for both sides, due in the main to the poor weather. However, the battles began again on 11 August with a series of raids ranging from Harwich in the east to Portland in the west.

The major attack of the day occurred mid-morning and was carried out by thirty-eight Junkers 88s of I and II/KG 54 against the harbour, fuel installations, ammunition depots and shipping at Portland. To ensure the bombers reached their target, a massive escort was provided by the whole of JG 2, JG 27, JG 53 and I and II/ZG 2. One of the escorting pilots was twenty-year-old *Lt* Wolf Muenchmeyer of 1/ZG 2. He had joined his *Staffel* on 14 May 1940 and had flown eight missions before France capitulated. Moving to Normandy, his *Gruppe* flew from a field flying strip at Ste Aubin where they carried out a few reconnaissance missions over the Channel with little reaction from the RAF. They then took part in the attack on the PEEWIT convoy before being tasked on 11 August:

Leutnant **Wolf Muenchmeyer, 1/ZG 2**

On 11 August, we went to Portland escorting Ju 88s, resulting in my first great air battle with hundreds of aircraft involved. Whilst I was guarding two Messerschmitt 110s ahead of me, suddenly a Spitfire approached from the side, pursued by an Me 109. I tried to avoid a burst of tracer bullets by lifting my port wing, this burst originating from the Spitfire aiming at me or from the Me 109 trying to get the Spitfire – I am not sure. In any case, I thought I had been lucky but then smoke poured from my port engine and I could not keep up with the rest and, looking around, I suddenly found myself surrounded by Spitfires left and right so I tried to escape by diving almost vertically at full engine power knowing that our Messerschmitts had a much higher wing loading than the Spitfires and therefore could get a much faster speed by diving. I calculated I reached 900–1,000kph, far greater than my instruments could tell me. Then, at sea level, I stopped my port engine and feathered the propeller. It took me an hour and a half to get back to France, my port engine having lost all of its oil and had seized. On that mission, we lost our *Gruppen Kommandeur*, *Maj* Ernst Ott.

It is hard to ascertain which RAF pilot was responsible for Wolf Muenchmeyer's early departure from the battle but one report is similar to what the German pilot experienced:

Lt Wolf Muenchmeyer, 1/ZG 2. (Muenchmeyer)

An unidentified Bf 110C of I/ZG 2 crash-landed somewhere in France. (Hoeller)

Pilot Officer David Crook, 609 Squadron

...Some Hurricanes were already attacking the Messerschmitts and the latter had formed their usual defensive circle, going round and round on each others' tails. This makes attack rather difficult as if you attack one, there is always another behind you. We were now about a 1,000ft above them at 25,000ft and the CO turned round and the whole of 609 went down to attack.

We came down right on top of the enemy formation, going at terrific speed, and as we approached them, we split up slightly, each pilot selecting his own target. I saw an Me 110 ahead of me going across in front. I fired a good burst at practically point-blank range. Some black smoke poured from his port engine and he turned to the right and stalled. I could not see what happened after this as I narrowly missed hitting his port wing. It flashed past so close that I instinctively ducked my head...

The RAF threw eight squadrons of fighters at the attacking Germans, claiming thirty-eight German aircraft destroyed for the loss of seventeen aircraft and fifteen pilots. German claims were exorbitant – fifty-seven RAF fighters for the loss of five bombers and seventeen fighters. Amongst those lost however were the *Gruppen Kommandeur* of II/KG 54, the *Geschwader Adjutant* of ZG 2, the *Gruppen Kommandeur* of I/ZG 2, the *Staffel Kapitaen* of 6/JG 2 and the *Gruppen Adjutant* of III/JG 2 – all experienced men who would be sorely missed over the coming weeks and months. Nevertheless, the German fighters succeeded in drawing their RAF opponents away from the bombers who successfully struck the oil tanks at Portland with numerous other hits on dockyard installations both at Portland and the secondary target of Weymouth.

The scene of battle then almost immediately shifted further east. The target this time was convoy BOOTY which, at midday, was just off the Essex coast. The bombers this time came from the specialist unit *Erprobungsgruppe* 210 which flew a mix of 30mm cannon-armed Messerschmitt 110s and Messerschmitt 109 and 110 fighter-bombers. This attack was undertaken purely by both types of Messerschmitt 110 with an escort from I/ZG 26:

Hauptmann Hans Kogler, *Staffel Kapitaen* 1/ZG 26

On 11 August, I/ZG 26 had to meet up with a fast bomber formation of Bf 110s over Gravelines and to escort them towards the Thames Estuary. Due to confusion during the planning (the *Gruppen Kommandeur*, *Hptm* Wilhelm Mackrocki was absent on this day and I was his deputy), we arrived three to four minutes late at the Gravelines assembly point where we found no aircraft to escort. I was of the opinion that the fighter bombers had already flown towards the target so I decided to head that way.

Somewhere west of Ipswich/Harwich, still without the fighter–bombers, we were attacked by Spitfires. My *Rottenflieger*, Oblt Wilhelm Spies, broke away and left me alone. Suddenly, I was attacked from behind by a Spitfire and was hit in both engines. I then glided from 1,500m to sea level and tried to fly east as I was not being followed. Soon both engines stopped and I was forced to ditch. The attack took place at about 1300 hrs and I ditched at about 1307–1310 hrs.

I lost consciousness and when I awoke, found the cockpit full of water and so I had to get out before I was dragged down. My *Bordfunker, Uffz* Adolf Bauer, had managed to release the dinghy from the fuselage so we both swam to it and got in. What followed was a hard time for both of us because we had nothing to eat and drink for the next four days. All such things as cake, water, chocolate and cigarettes were lost that night when

the dinghy was capsized by a wave and it was not until the afternoon of Wednesday 14 August at about 1600 hrs that we were picked up by two *E*-boats in the vicinity of Nieuport. By that time we were the best in our *Geschwader* at dinghy sailing!

Hptm *Hans Kogler (centre with cap) and* Uffz Adolf Bauer (3rd from right) *after their rescue, August* 1940. (Kogler)

Hans Kogler's injuries forced him to miss the remainder of the Battle of Britain but he continued to be associated with Messerschmitt 110s and ZG 26, eventually becoming that *Geschwader's Kommodore* in the Summer of 1944 before it was redesignated JG 6 and the unit converted to the Focke Wulf 190. It was his fate to be shot down and taken prisoner on 1 January 1945 only to be killed in a freak hunting accident in the early 1980s.

As Hans Kogler and his *Bordfunker* tried as best they could to make themselves comfortable, the final attack of the day was taking place slightly to the west. However, despite heavy fighter involvement on both sides, the attack on the convoy came to very little and, as both sides returned to base, the weather put an end to any further assaults against convoys or maritime targets. In fact, a new phase of the Battle of Britain would start the following day which would turn out to be the day before the German's planned *Adler Angriff* major aerial assault.

The weather on Monday 12 August looked promising so the *Luftwaffe* commenced its pre-*Adler Angriff* missions by an early morning *Freie Jagd* by III/JG 26 designed to draw up RAF fighters so that *Erprobungsgruppe* 210 could attack unscathed. The targets for these fighter-bombers were the radar stations at Dover, Dunkirk, Pevensey and Rye and, for the loss of just one fighter, III/JG 26 seemed to achieve this as *Erprobungsgruppe* 210 succeeded in putting three sites temporarily out of action whilst at the same time suffering not a single loss.

Maj *Kogler, Gr Kdr III/ZG 26, looks at one of his Gruppe's victims (a B-17), 11 April 1944.* (Kogler)

The attacks on radar sites were a new venture for the *Luftwaffe* who by now had realised the importance of the early warning the RAF was getting from radar of their impending attacks. Added to this change in tactic were, a few hours later, the attacks on the south Kent airfields at Lympne and Hawkinge with the sole aim of preventing them being used as fighter bases. Luckily for the RAF, these attacks did not achieve their aim.

As lunchtime approached, the scene of battle switched to the west as a massive formation of sixty-three Junkers 88s from KG 51 headed towards Portsmouth and the Isle of Wight. Their aim was twofold – firstly to attack the naval dockyard at Portsmouth and secondly to destroy the radar station at Ventnor on the Isle of Wight. The escort for this attack was even more massive being made up from the entire fighter elements of *Jafue* 2-JG 2, JG 27, JG 53, ZG 2, ZG 76 and V(Z)/LG 1.

One of the German fighter units new to the Battle was 1/JG 53, commanded by *Legion Condor* veteran *Hptm* Hans-Karl Mayer. Taking off from the forward airfield at Cherbourg-East, they stayed with the bombers until just off the Isle of Wight and witnessed the first of eight RAF fighter squadrons wading into the bombers and, if they got in the way, their fighter escorts which were holding off the Isle of Wight. *Hptm* Mayer spotted three Hurricanes attacking and setting on fire a single Messerschmitt 110 so he chose to exact retribution. Bouncing the jubilant RAF pilots, he set the right hand Hurricane on fire; shortly afterwards it plunged into the Channel. His *Rottenflieger*, *Uffz* Heinrich Ruehl, dispatched the left hand Hurricane in a similar fashion, even though the RAF pilot was aware of the attack and

Hptm *Mayer sits astride his Bf 109 damaged 12 August 1940.*

tried, unsuccessfully, to flee. The final Hurricane did put up a fight and managed to attack Mayer's aircraft before being mortally damaged by Mayer who saw it turn back, emitting smoke, for the Hampshire coast. Sadly, the smoke got thicker and, in a gradual shallow dive, the Hurricane hit the water and slipped beneath the waves.

As all of this was taking place, far above the *Deckungschwarm*, whose task was to protect the remainder of the *Staffel* from surprise attack, watched the drama unfold at the same time as they were scanning for any possible bounce:

Unteroffizier Heinrich Kopperschlaeger, 1/JG 53

After I saw *Hptm* Mayer shoot down a Hurricane, I noticed behind the *Staffel* a single machine. As I turned towards it, I saw that it was a Spitfire. He attempted to break away to escape; he then tried to dive away. At 40m range, I opened fire at him. He attempted to break away to port but suddenly I saw a white fuel trail and he crashed into the water. The pilot did not bale out.

The German bombers succeeded in their aims – Portsmouth Harbour was badly hit whilst Ventnor was off the air for three days. However, the RAF tactic of going for the bombers, albeit after they had attacked, paid off and, together with AA guns, accounted for ten bombers. One of those losses was the *Geschwader Kommodore* of KG 51. Five Messerschmitt 110s were destroyed (resulting in the deaths of the *Gruppen Kommandeur of* I/ZG 2 and the *Staffel Kapitaen* of 8/ZG 76) whilst the only single-engined fighter loss was that of *Hptm* Harro Harder, the *Gruppen Kommandeur* of III/JG 53. Again, German claims were high (thirty-six confirmed and a further seven possibles) whilst only eleven RAF fighters were actually lost.

As the day progressed, further incursions took place back over Kent but not with the intensity and ferocity of the earlier raids. Again, airfields were the targets and each attack was supported by heavy fighter escort:

Uffz *Heinrich Koepperschlager (right) with*
Uffz *Heinrich Hoehnisch*. (Hoehnisch)

Oberleutnant Albrecht Dress, *Gruppen Technischer Offizier* III/JG 54

In the late afternoon of 12 August, my *Gruppe* was tasked to escort a bomber formation in its attack on the airfield at Canterbury[2]. However, at an altitude of 6,000m I attacked a Spitfire only to be attacked a short time later. I had luck that my aircraft did not catch fire just that my engine and propeller reduction gear were hit so I was forced to crash-land. I had suffered shrapnel wounds and was immediately taken to a nearby factory; shortly afterwards, I was taken to Margate General Hospital where I was treated and, after several days, I was then taken to the Royal Herbert Hospital in Woolwich after which I was sent to the prisoner of war camp at Grizedale Hall in the Lake District.

[2]The Germans did indeed report having bombed *Canterbury Airfield* at 1830hrs, scoring six direct hits on three hangars, four hits on taxyways and eight hits on miscellaneous buildings in addition to three aircraft. It is believed they were actually attacking Manston.

Oblt *Dress' Bf 109 after its crash-landing.* (Dress)

As usual with many German pilots, the only aircraft they encountered were Spitfires but it is believed that *Oblt* Dress was shot down by a Hurricane flown by Flt Lt Michael Crossley of 32 Squadron.

12 August had turned out to be a arduous day for both sides but the *Luftwaffe* must have been pleased with the results, especially against the radar stations. Bolstered by these attacks, *Adler Angriff* would commence the following day, but the German meteorologists forecast that the weather would perhaps have the last word on when exactly *Adler Angriff* could commence.

THIS AND NEXT PAGE
Another fighter casualty on 12 August – the remains of Oblt *Friedrich Butterweck's Bf 109E-1 of 1/JG 26.*

An early morning casualty on 13 August – Oblt Paul Temme, Gr Adj I/JG 2.

As dawn approached on 13 August, most of the airfields in northern France were hives of activity and then, between 0550 hrs and 0610 hrs, the first bombers lifted off into a cloud-laden sky. However, the crews were not aware that, because of the inclement weather, the attack had been postponed and just after they were airborne, the message was passed. However, only the fighter escort heard that the attack was cancelled and returned to base whilst the bombers droned onwards unaware that they were unprotected.

Meanwhile, to the west another series of attacks was developing. Again, the Junkers 88s of KG 54 were the protagonists and were heading for the airfields of Odiham and Farnborough. A further formation of *Stukas* from StG 77 had their attack cancelled when they were half-way across the Channel. Again, as with previous assaults, there was a massive fighter escort but it failed to prevent the RAF from harrying the attackers, as one pilot remembers:

Leutnant Wolf Muenchmeyer, 1/ZG 2

Early in the morning of 13 August, we went to the region of Aldershot escorting Ju 88s. We did not encounter any RAF defence because of cloudy skies and we landed back at base very short of fuel and just before it became fogged in.

At lunchtime, twenty-three Messerschmitt 110s of V(Z)/LG 1 were tasked for a *Freie Jagd* in the Portland area only to be severely mauled by two Hurricane squadrons which cost the Germans five of their fighters with a further five being seriously damaged. *Reichsmarschall* Hermann Goering got to hear of this débâcle and issued the following warning a few days later:

The incident of V/LG 1 on 13 August shows that certain unit commanders have not yet learnt the importance of clear orders. I have repeatedly given orders that twin-engined fighters are only to be employed where the range of other fighters is inadequate or where it is for the purpose of assisting our single-engined aircraft to break off combat. Our stocks of twin-engined fighters are not great and we must use them as economically as possible.

Goering was a great supporter of the twin-engined 'Destroyer' but the RAF had quickly found its weaknesses, as had its crews. It was becoming evident that the Messerschmitt 110 was nowhere near as effective as it was thought and, as the day progressed, more of its pilots were to find this out the hard way.

Later that afternoon, another series of attacks developed in the west. Targets this time were the airfields of Boscombe Down, Warmwell, Yeovil, Worthy Down, Andover and Middle Wallop using a mix of Junkers 88s from LG 1 and *Stukas* from I/StG 1, II/StG 2 and StG 3. Again, the fighter escort was massive, made up from the Messerschmitt 109s of JG 2, JG 27 and JG 53 and the Messerschmitt 110s of ZG 2 and ZG 76. The RAF response was equally massive with ten squadrons being committed in one way or another. The attackers claimed thirty-five RAF fighters for the loss of seven bombers and seven fighters. Some of the bombers reached their targets but the results were poor. In any case, the majority of those airfields, like the majority of those attacked throughout the day, were not fighter bases and had little if no effect on Fighter Command's operations. This fact would have annoyed and upset one German pilot if he had known:

Leutnant Wolf Muenchmeyer, 1/ZG 2

In the afternoon again we were engaged escorting bombers even though they were diving into cloud and we could no longer see them. We were then free to look for possible adversaries and, by chance, we found them in the form of Hurricanes flying at a lower altitude. I was flying as rearguard to our formation of about eighteen aircraft and as I was diving down on them, getting faster, I was hit from beneath by a lone fighter which, unseen, made sport of this type of attack (diving from a great altitude, gathering speed, lifting his nose and shooting from beneath at the last aircraft before disappearing). Good luck for him and good luck for me (to have survived so far in the war). I was hit twice in the foot from beneath and another hit must have damaged the elevator controls. Unable to control the aircraft, we had to bale out and in doing so I hit the elevator with both legs and landed with both legs fractured and in a tree.

Wolf Muenchmeyer's Bf 110 before... (Muenchmeyer)

Muenchmeyer's *Bordfunker, Uffz* Fritz Labusch, also managed to bale out but fell to his death close to where the Messerschmitt 110 hit the ground. The aircraft made a twenty-feet deep crater which burned for nearly 24 hours. The crash was witnessed by at least one person:

...and after. (via Cornwell)

Mr M E Vane

On 13 August 1940 I was haymaking at Manor Farm, Chilworth. We had not heard any warning and did not know that there was an air raid on until we heard machine gun fire overhead. The clouds were low and it was overcast and we could not see anything of what was going on. By this time, the farmer had stopped his tractor and we all took cover as best we could underneath the hayrick being built.

After a while, the dogfight above us seemed to have stopped so one of the farm workers said he was going back to the village so I went along with him. We had reached halfway between our hayrick and the village lane when it all started up again but with added intensity. After what seemed an extra long burst of machine gun fire, there was the scream of racing engines which made us look up at the low cloud wondering what was going to emerge. After what seemed like a lifetime but was in fact only a minute or less, a burning plane fell through the clouds to earth, its wings appeared to be folded back along the fuselage.

The crash itself was not witnessed by the victorious RAF pilot:

Sergeant Leonard Guy, 601 Squadron

I was Red 3, 'A' Flight. The flight intercepted twelve Me 110s at Botley at 1625 hrs at 12,500ft. I followed Red 1 into action but lost the section in the ensuing dogfight. I gave two Me 110s a short burst each, tracer bullets going into the second aircraft. No other effects were noted. I then attacked another Me 110 from astern underneath. I gave a four second burst at the port engine and I saw flames and black smoke pour from it. Enemy aircraft then started to dive steeply towards the ground...

Wolf Muenchmeyer's comment about luck for both himself and the RAF pilot was only partly true. Despite his injuries, the German pilot did survive the war whilst Leonard Guy was reported missing in action just five days later.

Adler Tag's daylight attacks then switched back to the east, ending with a devastating attack on the airfield at Detling in Kent. However, it was not used by Fighter Command and the material and personnel losses did not affect Fighter Command at all. As with nearly all of the day's attacks, *Adler Angriff* promised so much but achieved very little; the RAF had just about survived and waited for the next onslaught.

In comparison, 14 August was a much quieter day for the *Luftwaffe*'s fighter pilots even if their bomber counterparts ranged the length and breadth of the UK. It was also thought that Thursday 15 August would also be a quiet day because of anticipated bad weather over the UK. However, reconnaissance aircraft began to report that the weather was improving so at mid-morning it was decided to launch a synchronised series of attacks from as far north as Scotland down to the West Country. The day was to be the busiest day of the Battle of Britain so far for both the *Luftwaffe* and RAF and afterwards would become known as *Schwarzer Donnerstag* – Black Thursday.

The first raid materialised off the Kent coast at about 1200 hrs when *Stukas*, heavily escorted by a number of Messerschmitt 109 *Geschwader*, attacked the airfields at Lympne and Hawkinge. The escort managed to parry most of Fighter Command's attempts to thwart the attacks and both airfields were hit, Lympne being the worse off.

However, as this was taking place in the south bombers from the Denmark and Norway based *Luftflotte* 5 were nearing the Northumberland coast intending to attack RAF airfields in the north of England. Because the return distance from Norway to England was well beyond the range of the Messerschmitt 109, escort was provided by Messerschmitt 110s of I/ZG 76. Each aircraft was also fitted with an additional ventral fuel tank and two wing tanks to increase their range and to ensure that they stayed with the attacking Heinkel 111s of KG 26.

One of the pilots flying with 1/ZG 76 was 23-year-old *Oblt* Hans-Ulrich Kettling; behind him sat his *Bordfunker*, *Ogefr* Fritz Volk. Both had been crewed up just before the invasion of Norway in April 1940 but Kettling had flown operationally with I/ZG 76 since the invasion of Czechoslovakia and had two kills to his name. What happened to both crew this day is still very clear:

Oberleutnant Hans-Ulrich Kettling, 1/ZG 76

Our orders were to protect the He 111s of KG 26 which would attack airbases in northern England. Since our Bf 110s could not reach England and return with standard fuel tanks, we had one additional fuel tank under the belly and one under each wing. The idea was to use the fuel in the wing tanks first then to discard them over the sea and to reach England with the belly tank as the sole handicap. This ungainly blister was a handicap enough – it made the plane several kilometres per hour slower and the unused fuel sloshed around, making steering and aiming unstable and since the tank was made from plywood, it was highly flammable. We were all anything but happy to perform our first long-range raid with our mutilated planes.

The weather was fair and sunny with a slight haze over the sea – a very typical August day. We were told that special precautions had been taken to avoid premature detection but at about twenty miles from the English coast, the first of several waves of Spitfires came in for a fight.

Our altitude was about 15,000ft and our formation disintegrated into *Schwarm*, attacking the Spitfires and keeping them away from the bombers which had to continue on their course. All around dogfights developed rapidly and I followed my Number One, *Oblt* Helmut Lent [Later to become a highly successful and decorated night-fighter pilot] who went after two Spits to protect his rear. I heard *Ogefr* Volk working his machine gun and looking back, I stared into the flaming machine guns of four Spitfires in splendid formation...

Lt *Hans-Ulrich Kettling, 1/ZG 76.* (Kettling)

*Volk's view in the Bf 110
looking forwards.* (Volk via
Guhnfeld)

Ogefr *Fritz Volk (2nd from right).* (Kettling)

Kettling's Rottenfuehrer
– Oblt *Helmut Lent.*
(Kettling)

Plt Off Ted Shipman. (Shipman)

Pilot Officer Ted Shipman, 41 Squadron

The weather on 15 August was fine but there was a fair amount of cloud between about 10,000 and 15,000ft. It was almost full cover inland of Newcastle. I was scrambled to 18,000ft over Durham at 1300 hrs – the raid was reported as 30-plus at first but this was later put up to 170 Me 110s and He 111s.

I was ordered to engage the Me 110s which were escorting the bombers. Turning in behind a flight of Messerschmitts, I ordered my chaps to form echelon port to do a 'Number Three' attack (which really meant three against three line astern). Before getting into firing range, the targets turned hard to port and came straight for us. I doubt if they had seen us for they didn't appear to fire at us which they could have done with four machine guns and two cannon in the nose. I fired at the first Messerschmitt head on at about 400 yards range with a short burst of two seconds. The target broke away at a very close range to my left and disappeared.

Picking up another Me 110, I tried a series of deflection shots at

Ted Shipman sitting in his Spitfire in dispersal at Catterick.
(Shipman)

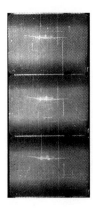

Shipman's camera gun film shows Kettling's Bf 110.
(Shipman)

various ranges with the target wading [sic] violently. No result and no return fire. Getting astern of the same target, I tried from about 200 yards. This was a long burst and the starboard engine was out of action with clouds of smoke. The Me 110 then made an erratic turn to port and disappeared into the cloud below, apparently out of control.

Oberleutnant Hans-Ulrich Kettling

...The plane was hit, not severely, but the right engine went dead, lost coolant and the oil temperature rose rapidly. I had to switch off the engine and feather the propeller and tried to reach the protection of the bombers which were overhead in close formation. I was not successful – the plane was slow and I could not gain height. Over the radio, I heard the boys in the bombers talking about my plane so I gave my 'mayday' because the Spits came in for the second attack and the kill...

Pilot Officer Ben Bennions, 41 Squadron

...I found myself about 300 yards astern of an Me 110 – I gave him a three second burst and the De Wilde appeared to be striking the fuselage. There was no reply from the rear gunner. The aircraft immediately dived for cloud cover on a south-westerly course. By this time, the recoil had put me about 400 yards astern but I dived after him, closing very slowly. He was travelling very fast indeed and getting closer to the clouds. I gave him another three second burst before entering the clouds.

When I came out of the clouds, I found myself midway between Piercebridge and Barnard Castle – about fifty miles from the point of interception. I reported to control that I thought I had just shot down an Me 110 in this area but didn't see him actually land...

Oberleutnant Hans-Ulrich Kettling

...This time they got the left engine, my *Bordfunker* and the front windscreen (the tracer bullets missing me by a fraction of inches). *Ogefr* Volk was lying on the floor, covered with blood and unconscious. I had no means of ascertaining whether he was alive or not. Since all flight controls were in perfect order (without the engines of course) and the belly tank empty, I decided to bring the plane down for a belly landing.

I dived away from the fighting, down and down, leaving the lethal Spitfires behind and looking for a suitable landing site. I eased the plane carefully down over a very large meadow but on touching down, I found the speed was still rather high. Finally, it crashed through a low stone wall which was hidden by a hedge, leaving the rear fuselage behind which broke just behind the cockpit. Looking back I saw the rubber dinghy, which was stowed in a partition under the fuselage and fixed with a long cable to the side of the cockpit, dangling behind along the meadow, inflating itself and following like a dog – a very grotesque sight.

The plane came to a halt at last. I jumped out, freed Volk and carried him to a safe distance, fearing fire and explosion. I disabled the radio with some shots from my pistol and I tried to set the plane on fire but the two incendiaries we carried for this purpose did not work as expected. One of them burned my right hand badly and that was the only honourable wound I had in the whole adventure.

After that, a lot of people (heaven knows where they all came from) came running armed with stick and stones, threatening and shouting from a distance until some red-capped Military Police took over and transported Volk, who had in some way recovered, and me to the police station of a nearby village where we were locked in two cells.

A doctor came and took care of Volk, who was after all not so very badly wounded, and he took care of my burnt hand too. We got an excellent dinner, with the compliments and good wishes from the local military big-shot. Several RAF officers came and asked questions and I think one of them was the pilot who shot me down. I went through these hours as in a trance – I only wanted to sleep...

THIS AND NEXT PAGE
Kettling's Bf 110 before...
(Volk via Guhnfeldt)

...and after.
(Norman and via Cornwell)

The attack was a disaster – I/ZG 76 lost seven aircraft whilst KG 26 lost eight bombers and failed to reach their targets. The RAF lost just one fighter – its pilot surviving. One of the luckier Messerschmitt 110 crews recalls what it was like to survive that day:

Unteroffizier Otto Dombrewski, 2/ZG 76

It was a black day for ZG 76 as we suffered such heavy losses. The *Schwarm* with *Hptm* Restemeyer, the *Gruppen Kommandeur*, flew at the rear in order to intervene wherever the trouble was greatest but they did not get a chance. Long before the coast, we were bounced by Spitfires and Hurricanes which attacked us in vastly superior numbers. We tried to form a circle but too late. The *Gruppenschwarm* was the first to be engaged in combat. We could see how they were broken up and *Hptm* Restemeyer shot down. We had to stay with the bombers and were in turn engaged in combat. Our circle of fighters was torn open and we were attacked from above and the left by a Hurricane. I asked my pilot, *Oblt* Uellenbeck, over the intercom to pull up to the left and we were able to open fire on the Hurricane as it turned out. She dropped away to the left in a steep dive, with a trail of fuel behind. When we got back to Aalborg in Denmark, we counted twenty-four hits – even the direction finding aerial had been completely shot away.

As this formation limped for home, the second and last ever major attack by *Luftflotte* 5 took place when unescorted Junkers 88s of KG 30 bombed the bomber airfield of Driffield, losing six of their number to a fresh formation of RAF fighters. The scene of battle then permanently moved back down to the south.

The first attack of the afternoon was by the fighter-bombers of *Erprobungsgruppe* 210 which successfully bombed the airfield of Martlesham Heath without loss. One of the escorting fighters holding back from the coast was lucky not to become a statistic:

Major Hans Truebenbach, *Gruppen Kommandeur* I/LG 2

Just off Ipswich, a British fighter pilot caught me at 8,000m altitude and put seven bullets into me from behind. Thank God all of them hit the inflatable dinghy which was stowed behind the armour plating behind me and so I did not spill a single drop of blood!

As this attack returned to France, Dornier 17s of KG 3 were heading for the airfields of Rochester and Eastchurch with a close escort of Messerschmitt 109s from three different *Geschwader* as well as a *Freie Jagd* by II and III/JG 26. The latter did particularly well:

Hauptmann Adolf Galland, *Gruppen Kommandeur* III/JG 26

The second aircraft I shot down on 15 August was at 1600 hrs, 15kms east of Folkestone–Dover at an altitude of 6,000m. Again, it was a Spitfire. Here our mission was a *Freie Jagd* west of Maidstone. When crossing the coast between Folkestone and Dover, we were bounced by twelve Spitfires coming from a higher altitude. Immediately, many individual dogfights started. I was able to get just behind one of the last Spitfires in this squadron without being discovered. From a distance of 100m to 300m, I fired with my cannon and machine guns until the Spitfire caught fire and big parts of it were flying all around, forcing me to evade. The Spitfire dived away and took a considerable time before it crashed.

The third aircraft I shot down on that day was again a Spitfire only seven minutes later at an altitude of 3,000m in the middle part of the Channel. I had assembled the *Gruppe* again just off the French coast. When flying back towards the British coast, at an altitude of 4,000m, I met some Spitfires beyond me. I attacked one and was able to approach him under the cover of his tail and shot directly into him from a distance of 100m. The aircraft made a half roll and remained on its back thus enabling me to continue firing. Sheet metal parts were suddenly all around and a thick grey-blue flame came out of the body and a white one out of the wings. After I broke away, the Spitfire was again fired at by *Oblt* Schoepfel; he followed the aircraft down and saw it ditch.

Another German pilot remembers this mission for another reason:

Leutnant Josef Buerschgens, 7/JG 26

After the dogfight during the *Freie Jagd*, Plt Off Ralph Roberts from Sheffield was forced to land near the beach at Wissant. Walter Blume, Gerhard Mueller-Duehe and I met him when we returned from the sweep over southern England. I was the first to run out of ammunition and was low on fuel and in the end, it was Gerhard who got Roberts. It was a hard fight and Roberts was very brave and an excellent pilot.

Lt *Josef Buerschgens* and Uffz *Luedewig*, 7/JG 26. (Buerschgens)

Lt Gerhard Mueller-Duehe stands alongside Roberts' Spitfire

Unusually, the 64 Squadron pilot was the first of three RAF pilots to be captured that day; the next two occurring about an hour later as the scene of battle moved yet again to the west.

Again the targets were airfields and two separate attacks were intended to split the defences. Twelve Junkers 88s from I/LG 1 were briefed to attack Andover, a further fifteen Junkers 88s of II/LG 1 went after Worthy Down whilst twenty-seven *Stukas* from I/StG 1 and a further twenty from II/StG 2 attacked Portland (with Warmwell and Yeovil respectively being the secondary targets for the *Stukas)*. Again, as with all previous attacks, the fighter escort was massive and made up from both Messerschmitt 109 and 110 *Geschwader*. The crews from II/ZG 76 had the task of escorting the Junkers 88s:

Unteroffizier Max Guschewski, 6/ZG 76

II/ZG 76 had been ordered to move to Guernsey and standby for further orders. Soon after lunch, the *Staffel Kapitaene* were ordered to the *Gruppen Kommandeur*, *Hptm* Groth, for briefing. The task for our 'Shark Gruppe' was to escort LG 1.

Take-off was ordered for 1400 hrs but half an hour before the scheduled time, it was postponed to 1600 hrs. At last the waiting came to an end and the Messerschmitts with the shark's jaws painted on their noses rumbled to the take-off positions. Due to the fact that the airfield was small (and completely surrounded by greenhouses!), only one *Staffel* at a time could take off. When all the planes of 4 and 5 *Staffel* were airborne, it was the *Staffel Kapitaen* of 6/ZG 76, *Hptm* Nacke with *Bordfunker Stfw* Kuehne, and his *Rottenflieger Fw* Jakob Birndorfer and my own turn to take off; after us the *Rotte* of *Lt* Jabs and finally the protection flight of three aircraft led by *Oblt* Herget. It was a beautiful, sunny mid-summer's day and the sky was the same blue as the waters of the Channel and there were no clouds at all. The *Haifischgeschwader* formed up in the typical shape of a wedge and climbing gradually it reached the ordered altitude of 4,000m. As we arrived over Cherbourg, in a huge formation LG 1 closed in from the south. Being one of its first sorties, LG 1 had the full number of

Bf 110s in formation. (D'Elsa)

Hptm *Heinz Nacke's Bf 110C.* (Guschewski)

Fw Jakob Birndorfer. (Guschewski)

aircraft whereas our unit had been properly fleeced during continuous operations in the French campaign and numerous sorties against England and consisted merely of sixteen planes.

After we had taken our positions to the left, right and behind the bombers, the whole armada moved across the Channel and crossed the English coast between Portland and the Isle of Wight. The crossing of the Channel lasted about thirty minutes during the course of which we had been followed by three Spitfires who kept a respectful distance, watching us from aloft. However, in my opinion, the attack on Salisbury Airport must have come as a great surprise for all the fighter planes were still on the ground when we approached the base[3]. Only when LG 1 had passed across from south to north, without dropping a single bomb, did the Spitfires start to take off in a most hectic manner, starting from all points of the compass! Whilst LG 1 was flying in a wide curve to the west in order to form up for an attack right from the centre of the sun, we were busy parrying enemy fighter attacks. The three Spitfires which had followed us came down in a nose dive, firing from all barrels. Meanwhile, the bombers went again over the airfield without dropping any bombs. We, the fighter escort, were all grinding our teeth because in the meantime, a great number of Spitfires had screwed their way up to our altitude and above and hurled down on us like swarms of wasps. The planes of 4 and 5/ZG 76 stuck to the heels of LG 1 who at last dropped their bombs and disappeared behind a huge cumulonimbus cloud in the south – Devil take the hindmost!

6/ZG 76 had no other choice but to get involved in air combat with an increasingly stronger growing enemy and I began to feel afraid that this might become our fateful day. First, *Fw* Birndorfer adhered faithfully to his task of shielding the *Staffel Kapitaen*. Only when three, soon after a fourth, Spitfires stuck to the tail of our Messerschmitt did he start to fight for our lives. Without speaking a single word, we both realised that only a miracle would allow us to escape our fate. While he tried all his tricks – tossing and turning sharply up and down and flying in narrow circles like a savage in an attempt to shake off the hunting pack – I emptied magazine after magazine through the barrel of the MG 15 without any perceptible results. We had lost sight of the

[3]The airfield was in fact Middle Wallop.

Staffel Kapitaen and we could not see the *Rotte* of *Lt* Jabs or the protection flight of *Oblt* Herget. They must have been engaged in hand-to-hand combats and they all fought for their lives. I am unable to say how long Birndorfer and I had been tossing about in the dogfight. It might have been minutes only but in my memory, it had lasted for hours. All of a sudden, I felt a fierce blow against my face – the thick rim of my sunglasses had been smashed by a shell splinter which then went into my left temple. Blood began to flow down my cheek and run over my life jacket. The same burst of fire blew out all the plexiglass panes in the cabin roof and the left engine was hit. Black and white smoke came out first and soon after flames spread quickly. The propeller of the blazing engine stopped and Jakob trimmed the plane and continued flying south towards the Channel. The pursuing Spitfires now followed us in single file and closed up to about five metres before opening fire. I could easily see the pilots and when they pressed the firing button, bullets from the eight machine guns hit our plane like a hailstorm – even today, after so many years, the terrible noise remains in my ears.

Soon the last of my ten magazines was expended. I could do no more than wait for the end. The plane in the meantime was so badly shredded that all the paint had come off and sheet metal of the wings looked more like a strainer but we were still flying. When we reached the Solent, my confidence that we might manage to escape grew bigger. But, alas, the ray of hope vanished with the change of tactics of the Spitfires. They now attacked us from the front. In the same instant, when Jakob had thrown off the cabin roof and both of us had loosened our belts in order to bale out, a full burst of fire hit the cockpit – we were both hit and I passed out.

Jakob Birndorfer had tried everything to get away, including flying through the Southampton balloon barrage but his two attackers, Plt Off Piotr Ostazewski of 609 Squadron and Plt Off Jan Zurakowski of 234 Squadron stuck with the Messerschmitt 110, firing when they could:

Pilot Officer Jan Zurakowski, 234 Squadron

After my first attack, there was no defensive fire so I attacked many times, firing short bursts. After every attack, I was breaking away hoping that the Me 110 would crash – the fuselage of the plane had a number of holes like somebody was sitting on the fuselage and attacking it with an axe. At one moment, I noticed another Spitfire attacking. We were approaching the Isle of Wight – the propellers of the Me 110 were rotating slowly. One warship in port on the north of the Isle of Wight opened fire and the Messerschmitt at fairly high speed crash-landed – some infantry soldiers were close to the crash

Plt Off Janusz Zurakowski.

site. Returning in formation with the other Spitfire, when the pilot removed his oxygen mask, I recognised the long nose of Plt Off Ostazewski.

Sadly, Birndorfer was killed – Max Guschewski regained consciousness to stagger from the wreckage and then collapse. The other Messerschmitt 110s of II/ZG 76 had to fight their way back to the coast, losing seven of their number – another fighter was written off on its return; a further Messerschmitt 110 from *Stab*/ZG 76 was also lost. To the west, III/ZG 76 was also mauled, losing three aircraft including that of the *Gruppen Kommandeur*.

Oblt Georg Claus, III/JG 53 (seen here with JG 51 on returning from his fourteenth kill, 12 October 1940).

THIS AND NEXT PAGE *Funeral of Cecil Hight.* (via Stebbings)

The day was by no means over. The Messerschmitt 109s of I/JG 53, who had also been escorting the Junkers 88s of LG 1, returned to their advance airstrip at Cherbourg-East and on landing, headed off for a debrief. It would appear that the Spitfires of 234 Sqn had fought a running battle with the returning German fighters. Plt Off Cecil Hight had been killed when his fighter crashed into housing in Bournemouth as he attempted to force-land in a non residential area whilst Plt Off Vincent Parker was shot down into the Channel and taken prisoner of war. However, Plt Off Richard Hardy found himself off Cherbourg and, it would appear, about to be shot down by *Oblt* Georg Claus of III/JG 53; Hardy was going to be the third RAF fighter pilot captured this day and the second to present the Germans with a Spitfire:

Unteroffizier **Werner Karl, 1/JG 53**

Somebody shouted "Spitfire!" and I looked up to see a Spitfire coming over the airfield. The anti-aircraft guns opened fire and the Spitfire banked around and landed. Having got over the shock, we crowded around the Spitfire. The pilot got out and surrendered to *Hptm* Rolf Pingel, *Staffel Kapitaen* of 2/JG 53.

The day was now coming to a close but not before the *Luftwaffe* launched two more attacks which cost them dearly. The fighter-bombers of *Erprobungsgruppe* 210 had been briefed to attack Kenley but in fact hit Croydon and the southern outskirts of London. They were then pounced upon by Hurricanes which shot down six Messerschmitt 110s and a Messerschmitt 109 with a further two Messerschmitt 110s returning home badly shot up. To add further insult to injury, Dornier 17s of KG 76 were

234 Sqn, St Eval, July 1940 – Hight, Hardy and Parker are the first three sitting on the wing to the right. (Stebbings)

THIS AND NEXT PAGE
Hardy's Spitfire after its capture. (Broeker)

briefed to attack the airfields at Redhill and Biggin Hill – the former was not a Fighter Command airfield whilst in respect of the latter, they bombed West Malling, an airfield still under construction and not yet operational.

As night fell, the *Luftwaffe* worked out it had flown in excess of 2,000 sorties, losing seventy-six aircraft against targets which were in the main not essential to the defence of the UK. The RAF had lost just thirty-five fighters but only eleven pilots had lost their lives – 128 German aircrew had failed to return. This waste of effort could not be sustained, especially as now it was obvious that there were no detectable weaknesses in the RAF's fighter defence around the whole of the UK. Furthermore, the much vaunted Messerschmitt 110 had received a severe mauling, losing twenty-seven shot down or written off on their return. It was obvious that all types of fighter mission were better suited to the Messerschmitt 109 but this aircraft did not have the range of the Messerschmitt 110. In any case, there were not enough Messerschmitt 109 *Geschwader* to go around and thus more pressure was being put on the already stretched single-seat fighter pilots.

If one thought that 16 August would be a day that the *Luftwaffe* would sit back and lick its wounds, one would be much mistaken. In the late morning, the attacks developed along the same lines as the previous day with airfields being targeted from one end of England to the other. The German fighters were heavily involved and lost seventeen Messerschmitt 109s and seven Messerschmitt 110s, which cost the Germans two *Gruppen Kommandeure*, two *Staffel Kapitaene* and one *Technischer Offizier*. The latter was *Lt* Richard Marchfelder who had a very lucky escape. His *Gruppe* had been briefed to escort a mixture of Junkers 88s and Heinkel 111s from various units which were to go after such airfields as Hendon, Northolt, Redhill, Brooklands, Gatwick and Croydon. He recalls that his main task was to look after the 'Croydon group':

Leutnant **Richard Marchfelder,** *Technischer Offizier* **III/ZG 76**

We started from Caen and I was on my way back to Lannion trying to get above 10,000m to avoid the 'Cowboys' at Tangmere. I was asked to look after two Ju 88s and it was a single Spitfire which did the damage. I attacked him head on but at the last moment, we both turned towards each other. Part of a wing or something hit my starboard engine; seconds later the whole wing was on fire. I dived, feathered the engine and cut the fuel to that engine and then set off the fire extinguisher. For ten to fifteen minutes, I struggled to keep the aircraft flying before the heat became unbearable and I told my *Bordfunker* Jentzch to bale out. He had difficulties so I turned the plane on its back and he departed together with the 'greenhouse'. I then had difficulties getting out and radioed that I was trapped – for this reason, my comrades thought for many years that I was missing and buried together with my plane! However, the next thing I remember, I was falling through the air but I did not open my parachute as I knew we were quite high up and had been on oxygen...

Both German crew survived the ordeal, even if Marchfelder did wrench his knee on landing. His *Gruppe* lost a further two aircraft with one crew being taken prisoner, the other being rescued from the Channel.

Earlier that afternoon, *Stukas* from three different *Geschwader* had taken off to attack airfields in and around Portsmouth. Met by a determined RAF defence, nine *Stukas* were shot down but not before they inflicted damage upon the airfields at Tangmere, Lee-On-Solent and Portsmouth as well as the unlucky radar station at Ventnor. 268 fighters escorted these raids and their claims were quite sensible – nine were claimed when in fact the RAF lost five. The German fighters had better luck when, in a one-sided fight, they shot down nineteen barrage balloons! Interestingly, during one of these attacks, three Hurricanes of 249 Squadron were bounced and shot down apparently by Messerschmitt 110s. No claims were made by any Messerschmitt 110 unit and one of the pilots, Flt Lt James Nicholson, was then awarded the Victoria Cross for staying in his burning fighter to press home an attack on a Messerschmitt 110; no loss of a Messerschmitt 110 can be matched to this incident.

Many of these fighters went back out again later in the afternoon, holding back off the coast waiting for the likes of *Lt* Marchfelder's *Geschwader* and the aircraft they were meant to be escorting. Some dogfights took place. 234 Squadron, who lost three aircraft and their pilots the day before, had the misfortune of meeting the same German unit again. *Hptm* Wolfgang Lippert of 3/JG 53, *Hptm* Guenther von Maltzahn, *Gruppen Kommandeur* of II/JG 53 and *Fw* Werner Kaufmann of 4/JG 53 each claimed a Spitfire. Fg Off Francis Connor baled out over the Solent, badly wounded. Fg Off Kenneth Dewhurst was more fortunate:

Hptm *von Maltzahn, II/JG 53.* (Schultz)

Oblt *Lippert, III/JG 53, 2nd from left.* (via Rupp)

Fw *Christian Hansen, 2/JG 53 crash-landed on the Isle of Wight on 16 August 1940.*

Flying Officer Kenneth Dewhurst, 234 Squadron

I was Blue Two patrolling with the Squadron over Southampton at 17,000ft. We met about fifty Me 109s. I turned to attack one enemy aircraft and gave two three-second bursts from dead astern at a range of 100 yards. Enemy aircraft dived steeply towards the sea. I was about to follow when I was attacked by another Me 109. A shell hit me. I turned towards the coast and then smoke started to come from the engine. After another two minutes, the aircraft was completely enveloped in smoke so I turned the aircraft onto its back and baled out. I landed safely and saw the aircraft crash in flames and blow up.

If the RAF was expecting a repeat performance of the previous two days, they were much mistaken and air activity over the UK was sporadic. However, 18 August would see the *Luftwaffe* renew its attacks with an added vehemence.

Apart from two interceptions against reconnaissance aircraft early in the morning, the main raids did not commence until early afternoon and can be divided into three distinct attacks. Firstly, a massive bomber formation thundered in over Kent heading for the airfields of Biggin Hill, West Malling, Croydon and Kenley. Accompanying the bombers was an equally massive fighter umbrella which was soon in action. The most impressive fighter action of this raid occurred near Canterbury when the *Staffel Kapitaen* of 9/JG 26, *Oblt* Gerhard Schoepfel, spotted Hurricanes of 501 Squadron trying to gain altitude to intercept them. Closing in behind and unseen, he shot down four Hurricanes in quick succession and only stopped his cull when oil from his last victim obscured his windscreen. During this raid and later that afternoon, on what would transpire to be the third and last raid of the day (targets again being the airfields of North Weald and Hornchurch), ZG 26 lost a total of fifteen Messerschmitt 110s with a further three returning damaged. In human terms, the day resulted in the deaths of nineteen men from this *Geschwader* and a further six being taken prisoner. Despite this, the following day *Reichsmarschall* Hermann Goering reiterated that there was still very much a use for the twin-engined fighter.

If 18 August saw another nail in the coffin of one German aircraft type in preference for another, following this day that aircraft was rarely seen again over the skies of southern England. The second major attack of the day was undertaken by *Stukas* against targets in the Solent area – I/StG 77's target was the airfield at Thorney Island, II/StG 77's the airfield at Ford whilst III/StG 77 attacked the radar station at Poling. Meanwhile, I/StG 3 was briefed to attack Gosport. As usual, there was a fighter escort but this time it was made up entirely of Messerschmitt 109s and of the fifteen such aircraft lost throughout this day, eight were lost on this attack:

Oblt *Gerhard Schoepfel (2nd from left) with* Lt *Heinz Ebeling (9/JG 26),* Lt *Josef Haibock (Stab III/JG 26) and* Lt *Johannes Naumann (9/JG 26).* (via Rayner)

Oberleutnant Rudolf Moellerfriedrich, 6/JG 2

By 18 August, I had only been with 6/JG 2 for fourteen days and had only flown one mission. That had been on 11 August when I saw my *Staffel Kapitaen, Oblt* Edgar Rempel, crash into the sea off Portland; all that we saw was the green marker dye in the sea and no trace of him was ever found.

On the morning of 18 August, we had moved from Beaumont-le-Roger to the airfield at Cherbourg where we refuelled. We were to escort *Stukas* in an attack on airfields near Portsmouth.

The crossing of the Channel was uneventful but worrying – we were all scared about running out of fuel on the way back. As we approached the Isle of Wight, we broke away. We saw three enemy aircraft – one at

Oblt *Rudolf Moellerfriedrich, 6/JG 2.* (Moellerfriedrich)

low altitude, another two higher up. Our *Staffel Fuehrer*, *Oblt* Gerlach, decided to attack. He went down with his *Rottenflieger* and attacked the lower aircraft. This aircraft did not crash so I attacked. My *Rottenflieger*, *Ofw* Wilhelm Laufer, and I followed and on breaking off my attack, I saw this aircraft was starting to smoke. As we had lost 1,000m in altitude, we started to climb back up. Then I saw a Spitfire – it was diving towards me and after separating me from *Ofw* Laufer, got onto my tail...

Flight Lieutenant Pat Hughes, 234 Squadron

As Blue One, 'B' Flight, I was on patrol when about twenty Me 109s appeared above me in the sun. I climbed towards them and my section was attacked individually. I fired a burst at one Messerschmitt with no effect and I then found myself attacked by two Me 109s, one of which fired at me at extreme range. I turned and set this aircraft on fire but was immediately attacked by the second Messerschmitt so I could not follow it down. He attacked and climbed away, then dived. I followed until he started to pull up and shot him with two bursts of two seconds each. This pilot immediately jumped out and landed on the Isle of Wight and his aircraft crashed there a few seconds later, on fire. When I had observed this crash, I saw a second cloud of smoke and fire just off the Isle of Wight which appeared to be the first 109.

The hunters in this case had become the hunted. 6/JG 2 lost two aircraft that afternoon – one is believed to be *Oblt* Moellerfriedrich's wingman who was later rescued wounded from the Channel. Rudolf Moellerfriedrich was not that lucky:

Oberleutnant Rudolf Moellerfriedrich

...I heard the sound of bullets hitting my aircraft and a volley of shots hit the left side of the cockpit. They smashed the throttle and wounded me in the left arm and smashed my left hand. They also managed to change the pitch of the aircraft's propellers. I knew that it was useless to try and get back to France so I turned towards the Isle of Wight and when over land, I baled out.

My parachute opened successfully and I proceeded to bandage my arm and hand with the first aid kit in my pocket. I did not see where my aircraft crashed but I was aware of the Spitfire that shot me down circling me.

I landed near a Youth Hostel I had visited earlier in the 'thirties and was captured by a Home Guardsman. I was taken to a hospital on the Island and later transferred to the mainland to another hospital.

Although the *Stukas* reached their targets, thirteen were shot down, three were written off on their return whilst numerous others were damaged. Coupled with the losses two days earlier, it was now decided that despite fighter cover, *Stukas* were not a viable weapon over the skies of southern England and were permanently withdrawn from the Battle of Britain.

Whether by luck or by divine intervention, the weather for the next five days restricted German air operations. The occasional fighter-against-fighter combat took place but kills and losses on both sides were infrequent. However, from a German fighter commander's viewpoint, these days were vital as *Reichsmarschall* Goering, infuriated by what he thought was a lack of aggressiveness by some of his fighter *Gruppen Kommandeure* and *Geschwader Kommodoren*, promoted many younger and successful pilots to take their places.

24 August saw an improvement in the weather and the start of the *Luftwaffe*'s new aim to destroy the RAF fighters either in the air, on the ground or, for that matter, where they were being manufactured. This day also saw a new tactic in that the *Luftwaffe* tended to roll one attack into another so it is hard to differentiate between attacks unless the region over which the battle was being fought changed.

Just as 18 August saw the demise of the *Stuka*, 24 August was to see the beginning of the end for another aircraft type, this time from the RAF:

Pilot Officer Eric Barwell, 264 Squadron

The Squadron was sent on patrol and after an inconclusive engagement, landed at Manston to refuel and rearm. We had just completed that but were not ordered up again until we were scrambled in a hurry just as a number of Ju 88s were attacking Ramsgate and the edge of the airfield. We took off in twos and threes but had no time to form up as a Squadron. I had one new crew in my Section (Plt Offs Jones and Ponting) and we chased after the bombers as they headed for France. It was a long stern chase and before we were near enough to engage them, I spotted five enemy fighters. I at once called up Jones, "Bandits! Line astern – evasive action!" and turned as hard as possible as they attacked. Unfortunately, Jones did not turn hard enough and was hit and went down immediately. All five aircraft then concentrated on me and as each came in, I turned hard giving my gunner, Sgt Martin, a straight no deflection shot. I saw strikes on one or two of them and one went down into the sea. On one occasion, Martin did not fire – I do not think I swore at him but asked him why. "You blacked me out" was his answer. We were some miles out to sea and it meant I had to keep turning hard as each plane attacked and I began to think that we should never get back to the Kent coast but the attacks ceased. (I like to think that we had damaged the four other aircraft but probably they had run out of fuel or ammunition.) We landed back at Hornchurch with no damage but the squadron had suffered disastrously. We had lost our Commanding Officer, Sqn Ldr Philip Hunter, who had been so good at welding together the squadron and at developing Defiant tactics, and two other crews. In the afternoon we were at readiness again at Hornchurch, sitting in our aircraft as there was so much enemy activity. We learnt there were bombers aiming in our direction but we were kept on the ground until over the Tannoy came the order "264 Squadron scramble, scramble, scramble!". Personally I blame the panic in the voice for the serious damage to two Defiants – they collided on the ground when taxiing. As the rest of us took off, the bombs were falling on the airfield just about where we had been a moment before. A formation of Heinkels was overhead at 10,000–15,000ft. We did not have a chance to catch them. I believe that one or two of our machines were attacked by fighters and we lost one, the pilot being saved but the gunner dying of wounds.

Pilots of 264 Sqn, 29 May 1940 – Sqn Ldr Philip Hunter is standing 3rd from left, Plt Off Eric Barwell is standing 3rd from right. (Barwell)

A few hours later, during another raid, it was the turn of a German fighter pilot to be on the receiving end:

Feldwebel Herbert Bischoff, 1/JG 52

I joined JG 52 in February 1940 and flew about sixty to seventy operational flights of which twenty to twenty-five were over England. I had just half a kill to my name – a Spitfire together with *Uffz* Ignatz Schinabeck between Calais and Dover on 11 August 1940. On my last flight of 24 August it was a Spitfire that got me – coming out of the sun above me. He hit my engine which was then *kaput*. I was at 6,000m near London at the time. I dived away but soon realised that it was impossible to get back to my airfield at Coquelles as by then even my radiators were *kaput* so I crash landed near Margate and became a prisoner of war for the next seven years.

Pilots of 1/JG 52 – left to right Uffz *Reinhard Neumann (+ 28 June 1940),* Fw *Herbert Bischoff (POW 24 August 1940),* Fw *Heinz Uerlings (POW 2 September 1940) and* Ofw *Oskar Strack (+ 26 October 1940).* (Bischoff)

A brand new 'Emil' for 1/JG 52 – Oblt Carl Lommel, the **Staffel Kapitaen** *(standing on the wing), is trying to get a pet cat off the exhaust stubs.* (Bischoff)

Herbert Bischoff's Bf 109 after its crash-landing.

As with many combats, the crash landing was not witnessed by the successful RAF pilot:

Flight Lieutenant George Gribble, 'B' Flight, 54 Squadron

I was leading 'B' Flight when the Squadron attacked about nine He 113s [sic] over Dover and itself was attacked by a large number of Me 109s. After a dogfight in which I engaged several enemy aircraft but was unable to see any results of my fire, I joined up with three other Spitfires over Manston and proceeded to Hornchurch. Between Manston and Herne Bay, I saw about fifty Me 109s in vics line astern. I dived onto the last section and fired the remainder of my ammunition (about ten seconds' worth) in bursts from 250 yards in astern attack. My last burst hit the starboard radiator and after that, the aircraft fell away out of control.

Pilots of 54 Sqn, July 1940. Flt Lt George Gribble is in the middle row far right. (Deere)

The crash-landing was not witnessed but the aircraft was heard and then seen by one teenager soon afterwards:

Richard Hambidge

My mother and I were in our air raid shelter in the back garden – we had been there for much of the day because it was quite hectic at that time. We were sitting and talking when all of a sudden 'zoom!' – it was so low, we never heard it coming. About half an hour later, our local air raid warden came into the garden and told us that it was a Messerschmitt that had just gone over and it had crashed out in the cornfields. He said he was one of the first to get to the scene of the crash and that the pilot was OK.

After that, I was off to see for myself. When I got out there, I was so surprised how close to home it had crashed and that it had caught one of its wings on the many concrete posts which had been put into open fields to hinder German gliders if they ever invaded us. The pilot must have been very lucky.

The final attack of the day appeared on Ventnor's radar screens, now just about working again, at about 1540 hrs when a formation of 100-plus aircraft were picked up north of the Somme Estuary and appeared to be heading towards Portsmouth. Forty-six Junkers 88s of I and III/KG 51 were briefed to attack the repair workshops and dry docks in Portsmouth Dockyard and to enable them to do that, a formation of 302 fighters, made up of both Messerschmitt 109s and 110s, escorted the bombers.

One of the escorting units was I/JG 53 whose task was to stay with the bombers, leaving the Messerschmitt 109s of II/JG 53 to go after the RAF fighters. The Spitfires and Hurricanes of No 10 Group were hurriedly scrambled and began to patrol, waiting for the arrival of the Germans. When they did arrive, the majority found themselves well below the German formation, helpless to prevent the bombers attacking Portsmouth.

As the bombers wheeled around and headed for home, 1/JG 53 broke away looking for prey. The Spitfires of 234 Squadron had been scrambled from the airfield at Middle Wallop and were in a good attacking position, or so they thought:

Pilot Officer Jan Zurakowski, 234 Squadron

I was Number Two in the last Section. My Section Leader was lagging too far behind the Squadron (probably because the Leader was using full power). I noticed slightly below us a formation of, I think, thirty-five-plus Me 110s or Ju 88s flying in seven vics of five aircraft each in the opposite direction. The position for a head on attack was excellent – I had good training in head-on attacks when in Poland so I decided to try.

I attacked straight ahead, slightly diving, at the last aircraft on the right side in the last vic. I reported later that I fired two bursts at approximately 400 and 150 yards. I could not see any results but think I was aiming correctly.

After the attack, I was trying to rejoin the Squadron in the hope that my Leader did not notice I was missing. I immediately heard a good bang and lost control of the elevator and rudder. My impression at the time was that the bombers had 20mm cannons installed for rear defence; later I thought it was more likely that Me 109s were hiding higher, in the sun, and were happy to attack a single aircraft hundreds of yards behind a squadron...

A lone Spitfire was spotted by the *Staffel Kapitaen* of 1/JG 53, *Hptm* Hans-Karl Mayer and it was he who chased after it. However, the credit for the kill went to another pilot:

Leutnant **Alfred Zeis, 1/JG 53**

We were on a *Freie Jagd* over Portsmouth and the Isle of Wight. I was flying as the mobile *Rotte* between the lead *Schwarm* and lookout *Schwarm*. *Hptm* Mayer attacked a Spitfire from behind and the aircraft curved left and *Hptm* Mayer was not outside of him. I came and was in a better position (above) to shoot. The aircraft went into a downwards spiral and crashed at a shallow angle on the eastern part of the Isle of Wight.

Pilots of 1/JG 53; Lt Alfred Zeis is 2nd from the left.

Although his report gave the impression it was over quickly, Zeis had to fire fifty-six 20mm rounds and a further 128 machine gun rounds to cause fatal damage to the Spitfire but he succeeded in his aim:

Pilot Officer Jan Zurakowski

...My Spitfire turned slowly, stalled and ended in a flat spin. I had to bale out. I was not sure which way I should jump – inside or outside the spin. It turned out later that I did it wrongly. I was descending faster than the aircraft and the Spitfire was spinning above my head and I was afraid to pull the ripcord. I was slowly gaining distance but the Spitfire was turning all the time exactly above my head. Looking down, I realised that the ground was approaching fast and when I could distinguish a man with a gun, I pulled the ripcord. My parachute opened fast, I heard a loud bang when the Spitfire hit the ground and a few seconds later, I landed close to this chap with a gun.

The old man (from the Home Guard) with a double-barrelled shotgun was shaken badly by an aircraft and a man dropping from the sky. I was not speaking English well so I was trying to show him my RAF identity card but his hands were shaking so much, he could not take it. A short time later, a British Army officer arrived and he cleared up the situation.

Despite the loss of two Messerschmitt 109s and a 110 as well as a Junkers 88 (which was a victim of AA fire), the raid was devastating and the loss of life was the highest in a single raid so far during the Battle of Britain. The German fighters appeared to have done their job well or perhaps the British Controller had put his fighters at the wrong altitude (probably expecting *Stukas)*. Nevertheless, the bombers had done their job but at the same time had hit the city itself; later that night nocturnal bombers would accidentally do the same thing to parts of London. It was a grim taste of things to come for many civilians.

Despite good weather, 25 August saw little activity until the afternoon – the reason for this is unknown. Suffice it to say, apart from a few massed *Freie Jagd* off the Kent coast, it was not until late afternoon that signs of positive German action were seen as, yet again, another formation was detected to the west but instead of Portsmouth, seemed to be heading for a target in the Portland area.

Thirty-seven Junkers 88s from all three *Gruppen* of KG 51 were aiming to bomb the airfield of Warmwell and, to help them do this, they were escorted by 214 Messerschmitt 109s and a further 103 Messerschmitt 110s. One of the escorting pilots was 23-year-old *Gefr* Josef Broeker of 1/JG 53 who was on his second operational flight of the war and even that was not meant to have taken place that day:

Gefreiter **Josef Broeker, 1/JG 53**

In the morning, 1/JG 53 had flown from Rennes to the operational airfield near Cherbourg. I was not due to fly that day but because one pilot from our *Staffel* could not get his plane to start, I ended up flying. After receiving our orders, we went to our planes. I flew the one marked '15' and as I was the most inexperienced pilot (I had come to the frontline in early August), I had to fly as *Katschmarek* to my *Staffel Kapitaen*, *Hptm* Mayer. Behind me flew two experienced comrades.

Below us I could see the bombers (Ju 88s) and their escort. We had to fly a *Freie Jagd* mission. It was an emotional feeling to see, all of a sudden, the English coast beneath us. The sky was blue – no cloud to give us protection in case of emergency.

Gefr *Josef Broeker.* (Broeker)

Broeker's 'White 15' just before the 25 August 1940 mission. (Broeker)

Our *Staffel Kapitaen* had noticed enemy fighters and ordered us to attack. However, it was Spitfires that attacked us, coming out of the sun. Both near and far there were dogfights. We attacked the Spitfires by turning left and the *Staffel Kapitaen* fired the first bursts and I followed him. Both comrades behind me broke away and had their own dogfights.

Suddenly, I felt my plane being hit. It climbed for a moment, lost speed and, inverted, dived away. I got into a spin to the left and there was no feeling to the control column. I saw the view of England, France, England but I could not regain control…

Pilot Officer Walter Beaumont, 152 Squadron

I was Green Two and we were at 17,000ft when we met a large force of 109s and 110s. A dogfight started. I followed an Me 109 down onto the tail of a Spitfire. As he broke away, I kept on his tail and got in a burst as he stalled at the top of his climb. I followed him down and on my third burst, clouds of white smoke came from the starboard side of his engine. He immediately prepared to force-land as we were at about 500ft…

Gefreiter Josef Broeker

…there was another hit to my plane and I noticed some pressure on my control column. I tried and succeeded to get out of the spin. I pulled out of the dive towards the Channel and I noticed that I was at an altitude of 1,000m. I supposed the engine had been hit (the airscrew was just windmilling) and was then engaged by three (or possibly four) more British fighters which cut off my retreat. I lost more and more height and looked for a landing place. By this time, the British fighters were lining up behind me so there was no chance of escaping.

I landed in a field and after I had regained my calmness, I set fire to my plane. I had put my silk scarf into the fuel injection pump and lit it with a match. The plane exploded and I suffered burns to my hand and face. I also suffered spinal strain because of the force-landing…

Pilot Officer Roland Beamont, 87 Squadron

I now realise that I was not the only chap taking pot shots at him. Such is the fleeting nature of air combat. I did record seeing another Hurricane above and behind me as I pulled away as he [Broeker] made his final diving turn to port and belly-landed off it.

Mindful of the need to stop him setting fire to his plane, I turned in for a possible strafing run and then, with thumb on the button, decided I could not do that. As I flew over at about 50ft, the pilot was leaning into the cockpit and then, as I looked back, the plane was on fire.

Plt Off Roland Beamont, 87 Sqn.

Hurricane of 87 Sqn.

Gefreiter Josef Broeker

...Two men approached me and said "Good day, Sir; how are you?". At this moment I realised that I was a prisoner of war. They both took me to a house where I received first aid. Shortly afterwards, soldiers appeared who took me back to my plane which by now was almost completely burnt out. From there they brought me to an airfield which had obviously just been attacked by the Ju 88s. Little did I realise that from this time onwards I would stay in British and Canadian captivity until 7 January 1947 when I was released and could go home.

A total of eight Messerschmitt 109s fell victim to RAF fighters but only two pilots were lost, one being *Gefr* Broeker. However, the Messerschmitt 110s of the three participating *Geschwader* were, again, not so lucky. Nine Messerschmitt 110s were lost, one being discovered deep under farmland forty-one years later. The crew were identified by initials 'MD' found on a handkerchief – *Fw* Manfred Dahne of 8/ZG 76 had been one of those German pilots shot down by the Swiss on 8 June 1940. A total of nine aircrew lost their lives and a further five taken prisoner. One of these prisoners of war had a very exciting afternoon both during and after he was taken prisoner:

Unteroffizier Siegfried Becker, 1/ZG 2

The mission on the afternoon of 25 August 1940 was to escort a bomber formation in its attack on an airfield. I remember it was a Sunday afternoon with very good weather. The bombers overflew our airfield and we started after them and took position slanted away behind them. I flew as the lookout for the twelve aircraft from our *Staffel*.

The first I knew that we were under attack was when my *Bordfunker* started shooting and screamed "Break left!" and we were attacked from behind and the left. The attack was a complete surprise and had come out of the sun. The dogfight then lasted ten or fifteen minutes. I noted that I had lost my wingman – his *Bordfunker* was on his first operational flight so had probably not given him warning of the attack. The Spitfires were now behind me and I kept turning as if my life depended on it! I flew fast – first to the right and then to the left and then dived from 6,000m to 1,000m. I was by this time approaching the Channel and for the first time I was concerned that we would not get home. One engine was on fire and I could not get the fire out with the fire extinguisher. The other engine was loosing coolant and I noticed that the temperature was very high. There was no hope of me getting to the

Channel so I gave the order to bale out. I jettisoned the cabin roof, rolled the aircraft on its back and we both fell out.

We both came down by parachute unwounded but my *Bordfunker* broke his ankle on landing. He was one side of a railway cutting and I the other. In the distance I saw a Home Guardsman so I tried getting away by running along the railway line. However, I soon saw British soldiers on a bridge over the line about 200–300m away. I was captured, disarmed and taken to a private house. I was later taken to Portland.

Becker had fallen victim to Blue Three and Blue Four of 609 Squadron – Plt Offs Geoffrey Gaunt and Noel Agazarian. The former's account of the action matches perfectly that of the German:

Pilot Officer Geoffrey Gaunt, 609 Squadron

...as I dived to attack the enemy formation, I saw an Me 110 climbing up about 800 yards in front of me, heading south. I dived towards him and he started diving. I followed him down firing short bursts, some of which appeared to hit the Me 110.

I continued firing until all of my ammunition was exhausted and followed him down to 3,000ft. I then did a steep turn to see if I was being followed. I lost sight of the Me 110 – during the dive I had experienced return fire from the rear gunner. I went down to about 500ft and while looking, saw smoke rising from the ground. I approached same and found it came from a crashed aircraft three to four miles south-west of Wareham. While flying around, I saw two parachutes land, one each side of a railway cutting in a field next to the crashed machine.

The Germans left having managed to bomb Warmwell and at the same time claiming to have shot down thirty-five RAF fighters. In reality, damage to Warmwell was not critical and only ten RAF fighters were lost costing the lives of six pilots with a further two being slightly wounded.

The day ended with a further raid, this time back over Kent. The Messerschmitt 109s of JG 26, on yet another *Freie Jagd* in support of the bombers, claimed seven RAF victims – in reality, 32 Squadron lost two Hurricanes to *Oblt* Ludwig Hafer and *Lt* Josef Buerschgens whilst the Spitfires of 610 and 616 Squadrons lost one and two respectively, Sgt Philip Waring of 616 Squadron being chased back across the Channel by *Oblt* Kurt Ruppert of 3/JG 26. Waring was then forced to land near Calais and was taken prisoner.

The next day, radar screens did not start showing signs of German air activity until midday when the first of two raids aimed against airfields in the east of England were detected. In both cases, the RAF fighters were dogged in their determination to thwart the attacks. The attacks on Biggin Hill and Hornchurch were effectively thwarted but the Dornier 17s attacking Debden succeeded in reaching and bombing their target. The RAF threw eleven squadrons at the attackers, including the Defiants of 264 Squadron. The twin seat fighters claimed seven enemy aircraft before Stab/JG 3 intervened and they then lost three aircraft. The claims by *Hptm* Guenther Luetzow, the *Geschwader Kommodore* of JG 3, and *Oblt* Friedrich Franz von Cramon, the *Geschwader Adjutant,* match the three Defiant losses.

Yet again, the scene of battle shifted back to the west on what would be the last major daylight attack in that part of the country for this phase of the Battle of Britain. For the first time in just over a month, Junkers 88s were replaced by Heinkel 111s when fifty-seven from I and II/KG 55 went for Portsmouth Dockyard. 277 fighters protected them, the vast majority being Messerschmitt 109s. Back on line, Ventnor's radar picked up the approaching formation and four squadrons successfully intercepted; again, accounts of the battle are vivid:

Oberleutnant Hans-Theodor Grisebach, *Staffel Fuehrer* 2/JG 2

It was a lovely summer's day when we took off on an escort mission over Portsmouth. It was so warm, all I was wearing was a shirt, blue trousers, flying boots with flares strapped to the top, a flying helmet and lifejacket. I also carried a pistol. I was leading the *Staffel* as *Oblt* Heinz Greisert was not flying this day. Shortly before I got it, I managed to attack and set on fire a Hurricane which was attacking an He 111; the poor pilot got his parachute caught behind the cockpit of his burning plane. If he had got out, his landing point could not be far from mine as immediately after, there was a bang and a smell of burning in the cockpit. I saw big holes in both wings and believe that I was attacked from below. I did not wait. I rolled my aircraft onto her back, removed the canopy and pushed the stick forward. I was then thrown out of the cockpit.

I pulled the ripcord when I reached a thin layer of cloud at about 600–800m (I had free fallen about 200m before opening my parachute)

and I landed in a hedge. I saw many civilians running towards me from nearby houses – some of them even brought me cups of tea! They thought, as I had no recognisable uniform, that I was Australian so I continued to act Australian! However, I then saw a military motorcycle coming towards me across the field. The rider knew that I was German so stood there and beckoned with his finger for me to come to him. I was then taken into captivity on the back of a motor cycle!

Oblt Hans-Theodor Grisebach, 2/JG 2. (Grisebach)

It is believed that Grisebach's victim was Plt Off Roy Lane of 43 Squadron who managed to bale out of his burning Hurricane both wounded and badly burnt; his Hurricane

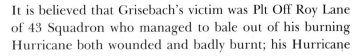

Hptm *Heinz Greisert, (right)* St Kap 2/JG 2, seen here as Gr Kdr II/JG 2 later in the war. *(Dudeck)*

crashed about two miles from where Grisebach's Messerschmitt 109 came down. Grisebach was himself a victim of a Belgian pilot from Lane's Squadron:

Pilot Officer Albert van den Hove d'Ertsenrijk, 43 Squadron

I approached the enemy formation head-on and fired three bursts at the leading line of enemy aircraft and then at successive waves from below without result. I turned behind them but was attacked by an Me 109 which hit me twice through the fuselage and four times in the wing. I went into a spin and when I came out, saw an Me 109 following a Hurricane which was diving steeply. I got onto the tail of the Me 109, firing whenever possible, and white smoke poured from the engine. I lost the enemy aircraft into cloud somewhere north of Portsmouth and cannot say whether I shot him down.

As this was happening, another German pilot was notching up his fourth kill, having shot down an RAF fighter on each of the previous two days:

Leutnant **Alfred Zeis, 1/JG 53**

The *Staffel* had been given the order: *Freie Jagd* over Portsmouth. I was flying in *Oblt* Dittmar's lookout *Schwarm* as the last man. The *Staffel Kapitaen*, *Hptm* Mayer, spotted five enemy aircraft 1,000m under us and attacked them. *Oblt* Dittmar, *Hptm* Mayerweissflog and I immediately attacked two flying a little away from the five aircraft. I attacked the right aircraft from behind and above and saw a part of the plane fall away. Black smoke was seen and the aircraft dived away and was lost in cloud.

His victim cannot be ascertained for certain but one RAF pilot fell victim to a German fighter in the same location to the north-east of Portsmouth:

Pilot Officer Richard Gayner, 615 Squadron

Plt Off Richard Gayner (left) seen as a Sqn Ldr with 68 Sqn, 1943. (Williams)

I crash-landed in a mess – wheels up, covered in barbed wire (presumably erected to deter airborne landings). I was covered in glycol, perhaps with oil also. I think that I had to side-slip from side to side to get a forward view through the glycol stream. Apart from the shock from being shot up and from the crash-landing, I may have been half blinded by the glycol. I was bleeding from the mouth and feared an internal injury but this turned out to be merely my bitten or cut tongue. My wife says that I also had a bit of armour plate in me from the explosion of the shells. I would have been in a great hurry to get out of the aircraft for fear of fire. I have no memory of whether I managed to get out myself or people came and lifted me out of the cockpit.

As the Germans landed back in France, they reported that they had encountered heavy fighter and *flak* defences off Portsmouth and not one mention was made of the target being attacked. The RAF fighters had done their job, for the cost of five fighters but more importantly, no pilots lost their lives. The official German records at the time state that four Messerschmitt 109s and three Heinkel

111s were lost. Post-war research indicates that KG 55 lost four Heinkel 111s whilst seven Messerschmitt 109s were lost costing the lives of six pilots. A further loss would occur a few hours later when a Heinkel 59 of *Seenotflugkommando* 2, whilst searching for survivors of the many ditchings south of the Isle of Wight, was shot down by Spitfires of 602 Squadron.

Over the next two days, the pattern of air operations would change. The fighters assigned to *Luftflotte* 3 to the west were reassigned to *Luftflotte* 2. The Messerschmitt 109s were re-based in airfields in and around the Pas de Calais. For the pilots of JG 2, JG 27 and JG 53, this meant that flights over the Channel were dramatically reduced, allowing the pilots greater time to operate and fight over England. These moves were staged over the next few days which, coupled with poor weather, explained why things were quiet on 27 August. However, *Luftflotte* 2 started targeting RAF airfields first thing on 28 August. One of the German fighter units had been rested from operations for the past two days and was keen for action. JG 26 had the task of escorting Dornier 17s and Heinkel 111s in their attacks on Eastchurch and Rochford airfields and had to fend off the attacks by four RAF squadrons. Unfortunately for one of these squadrons, after 28 August the survivors would take no further part in daylight operations during the Battle of Britain:

Pilot Officer Eric Barwell, 264 Squadron

Due to losses and damage, we could only send off seven aircraft and we took off to be directed at once to a high altitude. The Leader climbed at full throttle – we were flying in two vics with one (me!) as tail-ender – and the blue sky above was streaked with vapour trails. I told Sgt Martin to keep looking into the sun as I was confident we would get bounced. In fact this happened without warning. I felt something hit us and I banked hard, only to see an Me 109 diving down well below us. I then saw one of the Defiants streaming petrol and saw where we had been hit – through the starboard wing. I was not flying my usual aircraft and as we were in the process of having self-sealing tanks fitted at that time, I did not know whether this aircraft had them or not. Having turned when hit, I was now well below and behind the remaining Defiants which were still climbing at full throttle. I called up Control to explain that I was away from the rest, to be told to patrol over Dover at 10,000ft. I explained that I was by myself but the order was repeated so I flew a one Defiant patrol over Dover (and its balloons) keeping a wary eye on the fuel gauge. Fortunately, I saw no other aircraft, the fuel was going down normally (I assumed therefore that self sealing tanks were fitted) and I landed at Hornchurch without further incident.

Barwell was one of the lucky Defiant aircrew. As the Defiants struggled to gain altitude, they had been spotted by *Stab* and III/JG 26 who needed little encouragement to bounce them:

Oberleutnant **Walter Horten,** *Technischer Offizier Stab*/**JG 26**

From the airbase at Wissant, we set out in a *Schwarm* on a *Freie Jagd*. Crossing the coast, our *Schwarm* then flew in battle formation – that is far apart from each other in a line to the left. *Maj* Adolf Galland and I formed the first pair, *Oblt* Georg Beyer and *Fw* Straub formed the second. We didn't see anything for a while until Galland's plane started to fly a bit erratically and I realised that he had seen something. I looked in the distance and saw far off and at the same height a single Defiant which we approached from behind and underneath. It flew straight on for a while until Galland got closer to a distance of 200m (pretty close!) and opened fire. So did the Defiant with its quadruple backwards facing machine guns. I can still see the 'corpse fingers' (British planes used tracer ammunition that left white streaks in the sky) between the two planes as if it was yesterday. The pilot pulled his plane up and turned left and came across the front of my plane from top right to bottom left. I fired my first 90 degree shot with both guns at a distance of about 300m. I went in, fired the first burst of 20mm too soon and watched the trail of bullets go behind the Defiant's tail. Quickly I corrected and I could hardly believe my eyes. The two sides of the Defiant lit up as if it had been struck by a match and it plunged down like a flaming torch. I did not see if the two crew got out – I hope that they escaped unhurt as I

Oblt *Walter Horten.* (Horten)

had hit the tanks in the wings and not the fuselage. This lasted just a few seconds during which Galland and I were pretty busy and I couldn't see the two other members of the *Schwarm*. *Oblt* Beyer must have been shot down at this moment by Hurricanes which were lying in wait, using the Defiants as bait.

JG 26 claimed a total of five Defiants – three were shot down and five crew killed, a further Defiant force-landed and was written off. At least

Oblt Georg Beyer (seen with Lt Josef Buerschgens, right), one of the two III/JG 26 pilots shot down during the combat with 264 Sqn. (Buerschgens)

three more Defiants were badly damaged, one of these did not have the luxury of self-sealing tanks:

Sergeant John Lauder, 264 Squadron

We were ordered to intercept a gaggle of thirty to forty He 111s with masses of Me 109s as top escort. They were coming in over Dover and Folkestone heading north west and they had considerable height advantage over us. We were told to concentrate on the bombers whilst the Spitfires and Hurricanes took care of the Me 109s. We were endeavouring to climb up to the bombers when we were attacked by Me 109s diving vertically down onto us. I saw shells passing through my wings and it became evident that my petrol tanks must have been holed. The shells that had done the damage were obviously not of the incendiary type because there was no sign of fire. On checking the fuel situation on the fuel gauges, it was obvious we could take no further part in the action so I made for the nearest aerodrome which happened to be Rochford. After landing, we heaved a sigh of relief and were examining the Defiant for further damage when we realised that Rochford was being attacked by several Heinkels and we made an ignominious retreat to a nearby slit trench. We spent an uncomfortable few minutes there until the all clear sounded and then reported to flying control.

It transpired that we lost so many crew and aircraft that day that the decision was taken to remove all Defiant squadrons from day fighting and transfer them to the night fighter role. The next day the remnants of 264 Squadron flew up to Kirton-in-Lindsey in Lincolnshire to lick their wounds, take on new crews and to train for the new role.

A further bombing raid occurred early that afternoon (the three remaining serviceable 264 Squadron Defiants being part of the force scrambled to intercept it) but the day ended with a number of massed *Freie Jagd* by a number of German units. This was the sort of combat that Fighter Command wanted to avoid – of the six squadrons scrambled to intercept, eight aircraft were shot down and although they claimed to have shot down fourteen Messerschmitt 109s, in reality German losses were less than this. One of the German pilots, himself a victim, managed to score his last victory just before he was shot down:

Oberfeldwebel Artur Dau, 7/JG 51

I shall certainly remember 28 August 1940 if I should ever live to be 100! That day, my *Staffel* was on a *Freie Jagd* over the Channel and southern England. Suddenly, I had two Hurricanes in my sights and, with my *Rottenflieger*, attacked them. I had opened fire on the second aircraft when I was hit by *flak* over Dover and had to bale out. After landing, I was taken into custody by Coastguards and then a Bobby arrived and took down my particulars. Then I was taken to Folkestone and locked up in a cell. Shortly after, an RAF officer with a bandaged head appeared in my cell. We shook hands and he asked me if I had been the pilot of a Bf 109 that had crashed near Folkestone. I said I was and he pointed to his head and said "You did that!" I answered him "I am sorry"; then he left.

Some hours later, I was driven to London and interrogated. That was the end of me as a pilot.

Dau was probably the pilot who shot down Sqn Ldr Don Finlay, 54 Squadron's Commanding Officer of just two days; he was bounced and baled out wounded at about the same time that Dau was shot down. Dau was not shot down by *flak* but probably by Sqn Ldr Peter Townsend, Commanding Officer of 85 Squadron.

Ofw *Artur Dau, 7/JG 51 is taken POW.*

The RAF fighters had been taught a lesson on 28 August and were not keen to go head-to-head with German fighters the following day. Despite one attempted bombing raid later that afternoon followed by another massed *Freie Jagd,* the RAF fighters tried to avoid 'mixing' with the German fighters. Nevertheless, successes by pilots from JG 3, JG 26 and JG 51 were achieved but RAF losses were much less than the day before.

30 August saw an escalation of attacks which lasted virtually the whole day, one raid overlapping with the next in an attempt to swamp the RAF defences. The Messerschmitt 110 had been noticeable by its absence over England since 25 August but made an expensive reappearance on the 30th. The main raid of the day which involved them took place at about tea time when the designated target was the Vauxhall Factory at Luton. The Heinkel 111s briefed to carry out the attack were themselves escorted by II/ZG 2, II/ZG 26 and II/ZG 76 – the Messerschmitt 110s in turn appear to have had their own escort of Me 109s. Although the bombers managed to reach their target, inflicting heavy damage on the factory and its workforce, the Messerschmitt 110s were severely mauled by Hurricanes of 56 and 242 Squadrons. However, one claim was submitted by a pilot from another squadron who, by rights, should not have done so. 'B' Flight, 303 Squadron was on an interception exercise when, by luck, they ran into a formation of what they thought were sixty Dornier 17s and sixty Messerschmitt 110s. Against their orders, they broke away and in an action popularised by the post-war film *The Battle of Britain,* Fg Off Ludwik Paszkiewicz latched on to what he thought was

a Dornier 17 but was in fact a 4/ZG 76 Messerschmitt 110:

Unteroffizier **Heinrich Nordmeier, 4/ZG 76**

I joined II/ZG 76 just after the French Campaign as *Bordfunker* to *Hptm* Heinz Wagner, *Staffel Kapitaen* of 4/ZG 76. However, we did not get on well together so I became *Bordfunker* to *Ofw* Georg Anthony. We were escorting KG 1 in an attack on the Vauxhall Factory on the afternoon of 30 August 1940 when we were attacked by Hurricanes. They hit one engine which then caught fire. My pilot was also badly wounded – he had been shot in the stomach. Knowing that he could not control the plane much longer, he ordered me to bale out. I didn't want to – I was too frightened and still hoped that Georg could manage to fly home. However, he must have felt that he only had a few more seconds to live so he threw the cabin roof off, turned the Messerschmitt on its back and I fell out. The plane, still with the pilot on board, crashed about a mile further on. I came down on a farm with the farmer and farm hand waiting for me, shotguns in their hands. I sprained both ankles on landing and bruised my forehead.

Heinrich Nordmeier was luckier than the man that replaced him as *Hptm* Wagner's *Bordfunker*. In a fast and furious combat, Wagner and *Stfw* Heinrich Schmidt had the misfortune to be attacked by a Canadian pilot who had already accounted for two German aircraft that afternoon; they were about to be that pilot's thirteenth confirmed kill:

Pilot Officer Willie McKnight DFC, 242 Squadron

While patrolling with the Squadron over North Weald, enemy were sighted on the left at about 1705 hrs. The enemy aircraft were in a vic formation, stepped up from 12,000ft to 18,000ft. Attacked middle section of Me 110s and two enemy aircraft broke off to attack. Succeeded in getting behind one enemy and opened fire at approximately 100 yards. Enemy aircraft burst into flames and dived towards the ground. Next attacked He 111 formation and carried out a beam attack on nearest one, opening fire at approximately 150 to 200 yards. Port engine stopped and aircraft rolled over on back, finally starting to smoke, then burst into flames and crashed to earth. Lastly, was attacked by an Me 110 but succeeded in getting behind and followed him from 10,000ft to 1,000ft. Enemy aircraft used very steep turns for evasive action but finally straightened out. I opened fire from approximately thirty yards, enemy's starboard engine stopped and port engine burst into flame. Enemy crashed in flames alongside large reservoir. No return fire noticed from first two enemy but last machine used a large amount.

THIS AND NEXT PAGE
The remains of Hptm *Wagner's Bf 110.* (via Cornwell)

The day saw the RAF flying its largest number of sorties so far during the Battle – for the loss of twenty-one aircraft in combat and nine pilots killed. The *Luftwaffe*, in their biggest effort for two weeks, lost forty aircraft. Twelve of these were Messerschmitt 109s and a further seven were Messerschmitt 110s. The limitations of the Messerschmitt 110 were again evident and it would be another month before something was done for their long suffering crews. Until then, the suffering would continue, as many were to find out the following day.

The last day of August 1940 would see an even greater number of rolling attacks carried out by the *Luftwaffe* against such airfields as North Weald, Duxford, Debden, Eastchurch, Croydon and Hornchurch. The airfield at Biggin Hill was destined to be attacked twice that day – its ground crew had suffered one attack the previous day. This exerted an incredible pressure on the RAF fighter pilots who were now up against more German fighters than they had ever experienced before. Evidence of this is apparent by the claims filed by the various *Geschwader*. For example, JG 2 and JG 26 claimed eighteen fighters and twenty-two RAF fighters respectively on this date.

The day began early with Messerschmitt 109s trying to entice the RAF to battle by shooting down barrage balloons. It was the start of many raids and fierce air battles which cost the RAF dear. As these Messerschmitt 109s returned to France, two formations were plotted further to the east. These were Dornier 17s of KG 2 heading for the airfields of Debden and Duxford in East Anglia. Because of the distances involved, close escort was undertaken by Messerschmitt 110s of V(Z)/LG 1 and III/ZG 26. The Messerschmitt 109s of JG 26 were also involved but were flying to the limits of their range so any combat would have to be short and sweet.

The bombers succeeded in attacking Duxford and Debden but it was not until they were heading back that the German fighters were attacked:

Oberleutnant **Erich von Bergen, 8/ZG 26**

We were accompanying a unit of bombers attacking an airfield north of London the name of which I cannot recall. We had no contact with the RAF and in any case three of my *Schwarm* had turned back with engine trouble and I was on my own protecting the rear of the formation.

After the attack on the airfield and on the way home, I saw four Spitfires [sic] attacking us coming out of the sun. I was able to warn our formation and we turned to meet the attackers who overshot without causing any damage.

When we had reset our course for home, the Spitfires attacked again but this time from beneath. Although I saw them and warned the rest, they did not react. I turned towards the Spitfires and attacked the last one. Shortly after having shot down this one (the pilot baled out),

Oblt *Erich von Bergen, 8/ZG 26.* (von Bergen)

the first one got me with a full salvo. The oxygen bottles in the rear of the fuselage exploded and the fuselage broke. The plane could not fly any more so I gave the order to *Uffz* Becker to jump out and I followed immediately after. All of this happened at 7,000ft north of the Thames...

Von Bergen might have liked to have thought that he was attacked by Spitfires but his assailants were the Hurricanes of 257 Squadron. Three pilots claimed to have shot von Bergen down, the most vivid account being as follows:

Flying Officer Lance Mitchell, 257 Squadron

Green Three guarded my rear. I opened fire from 250 yards, deflection shot with short bursts at first until enemy aircraft more or less straightened out. Then I gave a four second burst. As I was doing my attack, Green Three informed me that the leading enemy aircraft were closing in on our rear. By this time, I had shot down the end of the Me 110. I saw the tail unit crumple and fall away and bits fly off the aircraft which went down in a spiral dive...

Plt Off Arthur Cochrane saw both crew bale out so it is beyond doubt that 257 Squadron got von Bergen. However, who von Bergen shot down is hard to say for certain. Plt Off Gerald Maffett was attacked from above and behind by a lone Messerschmitt 110 and his Hurricane fell away, the pilot baling out at 400ft but was killed. However, von Bergen saw the pilot of the Hurricane he attacked bale out and the two Germans and the RAF pilot were soon to meet face to face:

Flying Officer James Henderson, 257 Squadron

...All of a sudden, I saw two Me 110s coming directly at me, full throttle, line astern. Realising that I would present at easy target, I broke away. I flew straight at them and started firing at about 300 yards. I kept up the fire for five seconds. Both enemy aircraft broke away at point blank range, passing straight through my sights. First enemy aircraft must have shot at mine before breaking away as my instruments were shattered. A second or two later, the second Me 110 appeared and there was a great explosion in my aircraft as the fuel tank was hit, presumably by cannon fire. The cockpit immediately became a mass of flames and I baled out, falling into the sea three to four miles off Brightlingsea...

Oberleutnant **Erich von Bergen**

I was picked up by a Home Guardsman with a small boat. Though I was sour at my bad luck, I had to smile when he pointed his rifle at me, swimming helpless in the sea, and cried "Hands up!" Nevertheless, he took me on board. Later there came a boat that already had *Uffz* Becker on board. I came on board this boat which had a crew of two. They were looking for the British pilot I had shot down. When we found him, he could not get on board because he was badly wounded on one side. Becker and myself tried to get him on board...

Meanwhile, Hurricanes of 601 Squadron had managed to intercept the Messerschmitt 110s which had been escorting the bombers attacking Debden:

Leutnant **Karl-Joachim Eichhorn, 14(Z)/LG 1**

We had been transferred to a small airfield south of Boulogne from the airfield at Caen about a week before. On 31 August 1940, our *Gruppe* had to escort bombers attacking an airfield near Cambridge. Our *Staffel Kapitaen, Oblt* Michael Junge, was not flying this day so I had to lead the *Staffel*.

I can remember the *flak* from some cruisers in the Thames which was uncomfortable and the whole formation began 'swimming' from side to side. However, it was on our way back that my *Staffel* was

Lt *Karl Joachim Eichhorn (centre) with* Lt *Horst Werner (+ 13 August 1940) and* Oblt *Walter Fenske*. (Eichhorn)

attacked from behind by Hurricanes. We were flying at the rear of the *Gruppe* and my *Schwarm* (*Lt* Hugo Adametz and his *Rottenflieger, Fw* Jaeckel, as well as myself and my *Rottenflieger, Fw* Fritz) were at the back of the *Staffel*. The attack was a complete surprise and the first thing I recall was bullets smashing into my cabin and the aircraft. The right engine began to burn at once. My *Bordfunker, Uffz* Groewe, was shooting and crying at the same time. So to get away from my attackers, I dived from 6,000m to sea-level. There was some mist and nobody followed me. I now realised that Groewe had been hit by a whole volley and was lying dead in the rear of the cabin.

I was now flying at twenty feet above the sea on one engine and after ten minutes, the other engine began losing power and I had to ditch. Before I did this, I threw off the cabin roof and took out my dinghy. After touching the sea, the plane sank like a stone and I had some trouble in getting out. After some swimming and many trials (my flying boots were dragging me down), I finally succeeded in getting into my dinghy. After two hours, a boat picked me up and landed me at Margate. There I received some medical attention and a local reporter took my picture. The Commanding Officer of the local Army unit also gave me a very warm welcome!

Lt *Eichhorn after being rescued and landed at Margate.* (via Eichhorn)

Eichhorn's *Rottenflieger* was also not destined to get home:

Obergefreiter Karl Doepfer, 14(Z)/LG 1

The attack by Hurricanes was a great surprise. I can remember that a Hurricane came out of the sun and fired. All I could do was warn the pilot "Attack from behind!" and I returned fire and the Hurricane pulled away. I was sure that I hit him. My pilot [*Fw* Fritz] swung the Bf 110 away to the left and, at that moment, another Hurricane attacked and I heard the bullets hitting our cabin. We were by now separated from the rest of the formation and had lost a lot of height. My pilot began to curse. "The left engine is burning. I am going into a dive, perhaps the flames will go out. Prepare to bale out!" I pulled the emergency handle to jettison the cabin roof but it must have been damaged during the attack and I could not do so. The port engine was still burning and the right motor was starting to splutter. We were at this time still over land and my pilot called "I am trying to reach the Channel and ditch – try to jettison the cabin roof!" Thank God, it suddenly flew away and soon after, we ditched. Our Bf 110 sank. We were unable to free our dinghy. It was about two hours before a fishing boat picked us up...

The tail of Fw *Fritz's Bf 110 just before it was shot down.* (Eichhorn)

It would appear that Doepfer and his pilot were shot down by Fg Off Carl Davis; Eichhorn was shot down by another pilot:

Pilot Officer Humphrey Gilbert, 601 Squadron

I attacked an Me 110 which was being attacked by another Hurricane. It went down about 5,000ft in a dive. I had the height advantage and was able to overtake the Me 110 at full power. I opened fire from 250ft and the starboard engine was hit almost immediately and glycol spurted out. The rear gunner was silenced. The Me 110 went down in a steep dive to the sea but I succeeded in overtaking it again and attacked while in the dive. I fired at the port engine from which came white and black smoke. The starboard engine then stopped and the Me 110 was only a few feet above the sea. I heard repeated calls for help in German and heard the position being relayed...

Help was at hand in the form of III/JG 26 but they had been in combat with 56 Squadron; the only German casualty was the *Staffel Kapitaen* of 9/JG 26, *Oblt* Heinz Ebeling. He managed to shoot down one Hurricane before being damaged by another. He ditched and was rescued quickly. Despite his soaking and a bump to his head, he was back in action that evening, claiming another two Hurricanes.

The last day of August 1940 had cost the RAF thirty-eight fighters and eight pilots; a further twenty-two pilots were wounded. The *Luftwaffe* also lost in the region of thirty-eight aircraft. The outlook was bleak. The RAF could not sustain such maulings from the *Luftwaffe* fighters and at the same time were allowing their bases to be bombed by the German bombers. Some historians have stated that 30 and 31

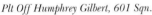
Plt Off Humphrey Gilbert, 601 Sqn.

August 1940 saw the *Luftwaffe* fighters starting to get the air superiority they wanted. The RAF pilots were tired and many of their airfields a mess and, if the Germans had wanted to, an invasion could possibly have been carried out. However, although the current German tactic would continue for a few more days, as we shall see, things would soon change – for the better for the RAF, for the worse for the *Luftwaffe*.

3
Maximum Effort
– September 1940

Despite the passing of the month, there was no change in the *Luftwaffe's* tactics. The initial raid of the month materialised just before 1030 hrs on the 1st when a massed formation began to assemble over France and then, half an hour later, crossed the Kent coast and headed for Biggin Hill, Detling and Eastchurch airfields and London Docks. The massive fighter escort would cause problems for one fighter pilot that morning:

Oberleutnant **Anton Stangl,** *Staffel Kapitaen* **5/JG 54**

At 1212 hrs on 1 September 1940 I collided at 7,600m with another Bf 109 during a dogfight. I remember the time exactly as I had looked at my watch just ten to fifteen seconds before the collision.

We were ordered to escort a *Kampfgruppe* which was attacking the harbour facilities of east London. We soon had contact with British fighters and my *Staffel* had been split up and each *Rotte* was having to fight by themselves. I noticed a Spitfire about 800m below me and I knew immediately that I had an excellent chance of shooting him down so I called up my *Rottenflieger* and told him to be ready to roll over and attack. Now I did what I always did before rolling over – I started looking back to the left and saw another Bf 109 of an unknown unit some fifty or sixty metres away with its airscrew shining in the sun approaching me at full speed. That look behind saved my life. I realised immediately that a collision was unavoidable, so I pushed my control column forward and to the right and felt a tremendous shock of the crash. My head was thrown forward and hit the gunsight (it bled very much afterwards but it was not serious) and I blacked out.

A few seconds later, I came to and I saw that my left wing had gone (giving me the best view I had ever had from an aircraft!) and a white fountain (either fuel or coolant) was shooting out of the engine cowling just a metre in front of me where the airscrew of the colliding Bf 109 had hit me. Now I reacted as I had been taught at least a hundred times during training. Waiting and thinking for a moment, throwing off the canopy and baling out (which was very easy from a plane in an inverted spin). I was thrown out with a terrible force and hit my left foot on the part of the canopy which was not jettisoned. I now fell through the air – a wonderful experience – and after waiting, opened my parachute. It opened at once at about 19,000ft and it took me half an hour to come down. The view was excellent – I could see much of the English Channel, Dungeness on one side and, on the other, Calais and the woods some kilometres to the east where our improvised airfield lay.

I landed in a barracks where British soldiers were exercising. I crashed into the top of a large pine tree and was brought down by a soldier who had the climbing ability of a most skilful ape. He looked

Lt Anton Stangl after shooting down his fifth enemy aircraft, June 1940. (Stangl)

Anton Stangl in the cockpit of the Bf 109 from which he was forced to bale out of on 1 September 1940; ahead of him is the gunsight that cut open his head. (Stangl)

Bf 109s of II/JG 54. (Stangl)

The badge of II/JG 54 (formerly I/JG 134 and then I/JG 76).
(Stangl)

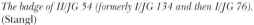

at my blood-soaked face and asked if I was armed and in my schoolboy English answered that I had a pistol and handed it to him. He shouted down, "Oh, he speaks fluent English!" which pleased them all! So I became prisoner of war number 51816!

Immediately after lunch, another attack materialised when Dornier 17s of KG 76, heavily escorted by all of JG 26, II and III/ZG 76 and V(Z)/LG 1, yet again went after Biggin Hill and Kenley. Like Anton Stangl that morning, another fighter pilot would end up prisoner of war because of an accident:

Leutnant Josef Buerschgens, *Staffel Fuehrer* 7/JG 26

For some weeks, I had been leading 7/JG 26. At about 1300 hrs on 1 September we took off from Caffiers. As with many times before, I was hoping to return there in spite of the many wearying incidents I had already experienced over the Channel and southern England. This time, things were to turn out differently.

Our orders were to escort a *Gruppe* of bombers attacking Kenley. Flying at an altitude of about 6,000–7,000m, we reached the target without being attacked and only then were we engaged in aerial combat with British fighters which were more interested in the bombers and the Bf 110s. I had remained with the bombers when, immediately beneath me, a Bf 110 flying in a defensive circle was attacked from behind by a Spitfire. It took no effort on my part to place myself behind the attacker so there in a row were the Bf 110, the Spitfire and then the Bf 109 flown by me. The gunner opened fire on the Spitfire and the Spitfire in turn tried to knock out the gunner. It was relatively easy for me to lay into the Spitfire in a continuous attack. At once, smoke started to pour from the Spitfire who pulled away, diving steeply. During the attack, I had got rather close to the rear gunner of the Bf 110 who was still firing and I turned away to avoid ramming him. At this instant, I felt an impact by the side of my foot on the left of the cockpit, the engine cut out and the propeller began windmilling. My God! The gunner had taken me for an enemy fighter (coming as I was from an acute angle from behind, I must have looked like a Spitfire!) and had got me! My heart nearly stopped beating with shock for I knew only too well what that meant. Trailing fuel, I dipped my Bf 109 slightly and started gliding towards the French coast, hoping to perhaps reach the waters of the Channel where I might possibly be picked up by a German rescue plane. The sun shone warm and bright and the seconds seemed like hours. I glided and glided whilst all around me furious battles were being fought. Some of our bombers which had been hit, fighters, enemies and friends fell, smoking, burning or disintegrating. Parachutes opened or didn't as the case might be. It was a gruesome yet thrilling spectacle. Never before had I been able to watch the fighting like now.

Lt *Josef Buerschgens.* (Buerschgens)

Gliding, I got nearer to the ground but could not reach the waters of the Channel. Near Rye, I finally disassembled my faithful Bf 109 into its many components. I regained consciousness in hospital, having suffered back and head injuries when I baled out.

Apart from another attack on Biggin Hill at tea time and an unopposed massed German fighter sweep over Kent, the RAF must have reflected that if the rest of September was going to be like the first day, the future looked grim. They had lost twelve aircraft and three pilots whilst the Germans had lost just seven fighters and just one bomber. Added to this, Biggin Hill had been bombed three times that day and the last raid of the day which had gone unchallenged caused even more serious damage to the airfield.

However, flying escort missions sometimes three a day was starting to take its toll on the German fighter pilots and most started to suffer from what they called *Kanalkrankheit*, literally Channel sickness, as one pilot recalls:

Unteroffizier Werner Karl, 1/JG 53

There was no talk about fear of being killed or taken prisoner. At least, nobody admitted if he was scared. All around us, we saw heroes both in the newspapers and on the radio. I think that everybody thought that he was the only one who was afraid. For example, our briefings were always held outside in the open air. Immediately after it finished and before we went to our planes, we all ran to the latrines and sat on the toilet. At first we thought it was sabotage but in fact it was fear.

Uffz *Werner Karl in the cockpit of his fighter.* (Karl)

Werner Karl's part in the Battle of Britain was to come to a sudden ending on 2 September. The Germans were quick off the mark with the first signs of activity occurring at about 0715 hrs when two formations were plotted off Dover and a third off North Foreland. At 0740 hrs the first German aircraft crossed the coast and headed towards Biggin Hill, Eastchurch, North Weald and Rochford and were almost immediately engaged by the first of six RAF fighter squadrons:

Flying Officer Alec Trueman, 'B' Flight, 253 Squadron

I was in Green Section when we were attacked by fighters at 18,000ft just before we closed with the bombers they were escorting. I did a very steep diving turn to get them off my tail and had straightened out and was climbing again when an Me 109 dived in front of me. I got on his tail at once and fired two bursts of about two to three seconds each, opening fire at 250 yards and closing to 150 yards. I saw another Me 109 getting onto my tail and I dived away. Each time I fired, bits flew off his tailplane and rear end of fuselage. The attack was near Rochester aerodrome; I had no time to observe if enemy aircraft came down.

The escort for the attack was made up from I and II/ZG 26 and I/JG 51 and I/JG 53, all of which lost aircraft:

Unteroffizier Werner Karl, 1/JG 53

At about 0800 hrs, I went to the airfield at Neuville with the rest of the *Staffel*. This morning there was an unusually thick fog so we did not think that a combat mission was possible. To our surprise, the *Geschwader* command gave the combat order as, according to the meteorologists and reconnaissance aircraft, this ground fog was only ten metres high.

I think we took off at about 0830 hrs – we still could not see anything because of the fog and dust until after we had taken off when, as forecasted, we went through the thick fog into the most wonderful sunshine. At once we formed up – I was the *Katschmarek* of my highly decorated *Staffel Kapitaen Hptm* Hans-Karl Mayer in the first *Schwarm*. When we reached the middle of the Channel, Mayer had to turn back due to engine trouble and *Oblt* Ohly took command. So then positions changed and I had to fly at the rear of the formation with another comrade and had to protect the *Staffel* against attacks from behind.

Our mission was a *Freie Jagd* in between 4,000 and 5,000m as a cover for our bombers which were attacking a target north of London. We reached the southern outskirts of London without enemy contact but then, after we turned east, I heard the warning over the radio that enemy fighters were attacking from the west. Because I did not want to be caught by surprise from behind, I flew a turn to the left and so there was some distance between my *Staffel* and me. Just as I was turning, I saw three Spitfires [sic] rushing down on me. Simultaneously, we opened fired but, unfortunately, I received a concentrated burst of fire into the back of the fuselage which destroyed my radio. My *Staffel* did not see all of this and flew on. During the dogfight with the enemy fighters, I was outnumbered and without hope and I received many hits in the cockpit. One of these caused a superficial wound at the back of my head and I lost a lot of blood.

I tried to shake off my opponents (by now I counted only two of them) by going into a power dive. At first, I thought I had been successful. I could not see any pursuer so I made a kind of inventory

of my plane. It looked quite bad so I headed for home. However, a quick look into my rear view mirror showed that there was an enemy fighter behind me in an ideal shooting position...

White 2 and White 10 of 1/JG 53 over England. (Tzschoppe)

It is thought that Werner Karl was initially damaged by Alec Trueman and if the German pilot thought that he was lucky to get away, his next assailant was not so obliging; for reasons that will become clear, that pilot had no reason to remember what was his twelfth of twenty-eight confirmed kills:

Sergeant James Lacey, 501 Squadron

According to my logbook, I had taken off at 0730 hrs and claimed an Me 109 destroyed in the Dungeness area which fits in well with Hythe where *Uffz* Karl crash-landed. I do remember that it did crash-land near a Do 17 at Newchurch. Later that day on my second sortie I again destroyed another 109 and also claimed a Do 215 damaged. My third trip of the day yielded nothing. This is the only time that I have ever had news of one of my ex-opponents!

Unteroffizier Werner Karl

...On instinct, I rolled over my right wing and dived again. I went down and tried to get rid of my pursuer by hedgehopping so it would not be possible for him to shoot at me. However, he was too clever. He flew about 200m higher and behind me so that he could get more hits when the situation was suitable. Apprehensive, I noticed that white and black smoke was coming out of my plane which meant hits in the engine and cooling system. There was a very strong smell of petrol in my bullet riddled cockpit – a fuel line had been hit. Now there was the danger of explosion the next time my cockpit was hit and my first thought was to bale out but that was absurd as I was too low. I looked back to my pursuer but could not see him but to my surprise, I noticed him to my right just above me. I do not know why he did not shoot me down – I was completely defenceless. Either he had no ammunition left or he thought it was not necessary any more. It was obvious that my flight was coming to an end and I only hoped that it would be possible to ditch in the Channel. This hope was in vain as after I had pulled my plane over rising ground, my engine stopped, perhaps due to overheating. I could see the sea but could not reach it and had to make a forced-landing on the beach. My right wing was torn off by one of those obstacles to prevent airborne landings. I managed to get out of the cockpit before I fainted.

When I regained consciousness, I was lying on a bed in a hut. Soldiers had given me first aid as I had crash-landed near to their living quarters. Later they told me they thought that I was going to crash into their hut. After I got up and could stand on my own two

Werner Karl's White 14 – the aircraft in which he was shot down on 2 September 1940. (Karl)

feet, I was allowed to go down to the beach. At the water's edge, I sat down and looked across the Channel towards France. For the first time I now realised that I was a prisoner of war. A short time later, a young lieutenant came to me. In very good German he told me that I would be taken to a hospital in a short time. He tried to cheer me up and I said I should be happy being in captivity and still living – I would survive the war but he was not so sure about his fate.

Although Werner Karl could not see it, out in the Channel another one of his comrades was also in trouble:

Feldwebel Heinrich Hoehnisch, 1/JG 53

It was one of those days in the Summer of 1940 when we had to fly to England nearly every day. On this day, there was a thick yellow-brown haze in the sky and the horizon could not be seen. *Uffz* Heinrich Ruehl reported engine failure so he was flying back to France on his own. I then heard him saying "I can't stand it in my plane any longer," to which someone said "Throw off your canopy roof." I was also on my way back to France – I always looked around to make sure of enemy attacks. I did not want to be shot down by one of those British pilots which specialised in catching lonely German planes. We called them *Leichenfledderer* – one who robs corpses!

Fw *Heinrich Hoehnisch.* (Hoehnisch)

In the distance, I saw a small dot with a black line after it and when I came nearer, I realised that it was one of our fighters with black smoke coming out of the engine. The pilot sat in his open canopy – it was Ruehl. I then flew alongside him, waved my hand and waggled my wings. I flew above him to make sure that he was not attacked but we were now at 1,800m and he was still losing height. The engine of his plane was still running but very slowly. The French coast was visible in the haze but he was too low. His plane's shadow on the water came nearer and nearer and a fountain of spray appeared in the sea and the Messerschmitt could not longer be seen. Suddenly, the tail broke to the surface and I saw Ruehl in the water. Immediately, the water around him was coloured yellow. I flew around and over the spot to make sure that he was still alive and then headed for France. My red fuel warning light had been burning for about five minutes but nearer the coast, I saw a motor torpedo boat. In cases of emergency, we were told to fly over these ships and waggle our wings and then fly in the direction of the emergency. So I flew back to Ruehl and then back again and tried to correct the boat's course. Then I saw a Do 18 with Red Cross markings and I knew that it would get to Ruehl quicker than the boat so I showed the pilot the direction and could see him land near Ruehl before I had to turn back on the last drops of fuel.

Uffz *Heinrich Ruehl (right) with his* Staffel Kapitaen, Oblt *Hans Ohly.*

Another fighter *Staffel* suffered badly at the hands of 54 Squadron who carried out a very successful bounce on 1/JG 51. Commanded by *Oblt* Hermann-Friedrich Joppien, who achieved seventy kills by the time of his death just under a year later, in its ranks were *Fw* Heinz Baer, who by the end of the war achieved 221 kills, and *Uffz* Erwin Fleig, who had shot down sixty-six enemy aircraft by the time he was taken prisoner in May 1942. *Lt* Guenther Ruttkowski was the only pilot to die when he was shot down by Flt Lt George Gribble. The future ace *Fw* Heinz Baer's plane was so badly damaged that he was forced to ditch in the Channel but later rescued. Only one pilot was taken prisoner:

Leutnant Helmut Thoerl, 1/JG 51

The weather was clear as we headed back to France to our base at St Omer. Suddenly, I heard a noise as if you drop some peas on a plate and at the same moment, my cockpit filled with blue smoke. I looked into my mirror and saw a fighter directly behind me but I could not recognise whether it was a Spitfire or a 109. If it was a Spitfire, I only had one chance – push the stick forwards and give my plane full power. We knew that the engine of a Spitfire had a carburettor and caused the engine to stutter when you pushed the stick forwards. The Bf 109 had fuel injection and the engine did not stutter in such manoeuvres. However, it was useless because my plane began to burn so I had to bale out at full speed as I could not close the throttle. After many efforts I succeeded and landed by parachute, with a burnt face and hands, in a meadow where many people were waiting for me. I was taken prisoner by Home Guards and taken to a nearby hospital.

Lt *Helmut Thoerl.* (Thoerl)

In a letter to Helmut Thoerl's father written later that same day, the *Staffel Kapitaen* tried to paint a rosy picture after having lost three aircraft:

Oberleutnant Hermann-Friedrich Joppien, *Staffel Kapitaen* 1/JG 51

In this mission, which brought us the loss of your son, the *Staffel* was attacked from above and behind by Spitfires. Your son got left behind and we could not help him in time. I saw that his left wing was hit and pieces of it broke off because of the concentrated fire of the Spitfires. I saw him throw away the cabin roof and am sure he intended baling out. The Spitfire was then shot down in flames by *Uffz* Fleig. I hope that your son is unwounded and a prisoner.

Oblt *Hermann-Friedrich Joppien,* Staffel Kapitaen *of 1/JG 51.*

No Spitfires were lost by 54 Squadron as the pilot who probably shot down Helmut Thoerl proves:

Squadron Leader James Leathart, 54 Squadron

Enemy were sighted over Ashford when we were over Sheppey at 20,000ft. I climbed a further 5,000ft and attacked Number Five in a vic of five Me 109s. There was no result. I dived away, pulled up vertically under the second formation of five, firing at the flank aircraft with full deflection. He dropped vertically and exploded on hitting the ground.

In addition to the Messerschmitt 109s lost that morning, three Messerschmitt 110s were lost from I and II/ZG 26; during the next raid at lunchtime aimed at the airfields of Detling and Eastchurch, another two Messerschmitt 110s were lost and, by the end of the day, a total of seven Messerschmitt 110s were either lying in British fields, at the bottom of the Channel or wrecked in France. Messerschmitt 109 losses were also heavy with fifteen being lost. RAF casualties were about the same, many being lost in the furious dogfights that occurred over Kent during the afternoon. The Polish pilots of 303 Squadron, recently declared fully operational and on their second major combat, narrowly avoided disaster when they were bounced over Dover, the bounce being spotted by one of the 'weavers'. Aggressive to the end, they chased the Germans back to France and only turned away when shot at by German *flak*.

Attacks against airfields continued on 3 September. North Weald was heavily bombed but remained operational. Fierce dogfights took place over the Essex area with, surprisingly, the Messerschmitt 110s performing well enough to keep the RAF fighters away from the bombers. Together with JG 26, they inflicted heavy losses on the RAF that morning, the Messerschmitt 109s holding back off the coast and successfully bouncing a number of British fighters, albeit the claims were too high compared to what the RAF actually lost. Two claims that can be substantiated were made by the *Gruppen Kommandeur* of II/JG 26 *Hptm* Erich Bode who bounced 603 Squadron off Margate. One of the two pilots shot down was Plt Off Richard Hillary who, in his book *The Last Enemy*, recalls vividly what happened next:

Pilot Officer Richard Hillary, 603 Squadron

...I felt a terrific explosion which knocked the control column from my hand and the whole machine quivered like a stricken animal. In a second, the cockpit was a mass of flames; instinctively, I reached up to open the hood. It would not move. I tore off my straps and managed to force it back but this took time and when I dropped back in the seat and reached for the stick in an effort to turn the plane on its back, the heat was so intense I could feel myself going. I remember a second of sharp agony, remember thinking "This is it" and putting both hands to my eyes. Then I passed out.

Hillary managed to fall away from his Spitfire, very badly burned. By luck, all of this had been seen from the ground:

Chris Fright

On 3 September, a Spitfire was seen to crash into the sea off Margate. The pilot baled out. The Margate lifeboat was launched and after a long search, found the pilot badly burnt. My old friend Harry Sandwell held him in his arms all the way back to the coast; Harry was very proud of this until the day he [Harry] died.

Even though it was not obvious to both sides, the *Luftwaffe* was continuing to achieve and improve their air superiority over southern England. The RAF continued to inflict damage on *Luftwaffe* fighters and bombers but the Germans had many more replacements. The RAF was struggling to replace both aircraft and pilots. Their airfields and aircraft manufacturing works were also being bombed; time after time the German bombers were getting through. However, 4 September would give the exhausted RAF pilots a well-deserved morale boost.

Aerial activity on 4 September started in the mid-morning with fighter sweeps – the results of which were inevitable for those RAF squadrons tasked to intercept. Two Spitfires were shot down, with one pilot fatally wounded, as well as three Hurricanes with two pilots missing. German losses were just three Messerschmitt 109s with one pilot killed and one missing. Under cover of the German fighters, Dornier 17s went after the airfields of Rochford, Lympne and Eastchurch, dropped their bombs and returned without loss.

However, early in the afternoon, a massive formation of 300-plus aircraft was plotted, one group going after airfields and aircraft factories in the Kent region whilst another, consisting entirely of Messerschmitt 110 fighter-bombers of *Erprobungsgruppe* 210 and escorted by Messerschmitt 110s of ZG 2, ZG 76 and V(Z)/LG 1, headed for the Vickers Aircraft Factory at Brooklands in Surrey.

The attack did not start well. On seeing RAF fighters climbing towards them, the *Gruppen Kommandeur* of the fighter-bombers attempted a manoeuvre which had fatal consequences – his plane hit the Channel taking him and his *Bordfunker* to their deaths. Shortly afterwards, the RAF fighters pounced:

Unteroffizier Adolf Kaeser, 7/ZG 76

During the briefing on 4 September, the question arose as to who would fly with whom. I was assigned to fly with *Oblt* Muenich of 8 *Staffel*. Our instructions were this: take off at lunch time, climb to 3,000m. At this altitude, we were to wait for a formation of bomb-carrying Bf 110s. Together with them we were to fly as escort along the English coast to a target near London.

All was done as ordered but hardly had we crossed the coast, presumably in the area of Brighton, when I saw fighters climbing in the distance to the west. Either the *Kommandeur* had not seen them yet or, which is more likely, he had strict orders not to leave the bombers alone. However, the enemy was so quickly above us and soon Willy, my *Staffelkamerad*, had one on his tail. At once I told my pilot and told him of the Englishman's position because we were in a favourable position for an attack. He did not react but held his course, flew straight on and after a short while, I did not see either a friend or an enemy. I had a bad feeling because I could not see what was going on below. I was vigilant but soon it happened...

Unseen by the German crew, Plt Off Pat Horton and Sgt Zygmunt Klein of 234 Squadron succeeded in getting behind the Messerschmitt 110 and managed to hit the starboard engine. They then watched the rest of the drama unfold:

Unteroffizier Adolf Kaeser

...clouds of smoke were coming from the right engine. Now *Oblt* Muenich tried to extinguish the fire by going into a dive. As a result of this, the wing was covered in flames. The airspeed indicator registered a speed which was well over the warning line set at 760kph. Then, the left engine began to give off smoke. No doubt this was the end.

Muenich pulled the aircraft out of the dive and I told him that I was going to bale out so I pulled the cockpit hood jettisoning lever but nothing happened. Now I went forward to the radio equipment and pulled the lever that was there – the hood did not move. Then I got on the seat and pressed my back against the hood – nothing! Now I told Muenich that I was not able to get out of the plane so he stayed with the plane and headed for the coast. Suddenly, just before landing, the hood flew off but now it was too late to bale out.

Just before the aircraft landed, the pilot side-slipped to the left and the wing hit the ground and was compressed like an accordion. This way the force of the impact was reduced considerably. I only saw that the left engine was ripped out of its engine bearers and was rolling down the slope. Then I blacked out. When I came to my senses again, my head was throbbing – I had a scratch on my left temple. Then an old gentleman appeared next to me as if by magic as I had not seen any buildings from above and this area seemed to be deserted. I asked him how far it was to the coast. "Twelve miles," he replied. Then he left. I took the dinghy out of its stowage and together with *Oblt* Muenich quickly left the burning aircraft. We had hardly gone about 100m when there were explosions – the fire had reached the ammunition.

I could still not get the old man out of my mind – where did he come from and what was he doing here? I was soon to find out. We went through some bushes and after taking a few steps stopped – in the middle of a clearing there were some people on a blanket having a picnic. It was an idyllic sight but how could we pass them unseen? We had planned to make for the coast and to launch our dinghy under cover of darkness, hoping to be picked up by German air-sea rescue aircraft the next morning. Then I heard the sound of engines coming nearer. Soon we could see through a less dense part of the wood some military vehicles stopping not far from us. Now I was aware of the old man's role – I guess he was from the Observer Corps and had phoned and informed the military. That was a neat bit of work!

Because I still had my pistol, I put it under some moss and waited to see what would happen. We saw soldiers with rifles fanning out who, in an extended line, were heading towards us. So we went into captivity. After we had been captured, the commanding officer asked us if we wanted a souvenir from our aircraft. I thought that was a noble gesture.

The remains of Adolf Kaeser's Bf 110. (Cornwell)

The German formation had to run the gauntlet of at least two lines of defence before the bombers reached their target. Despite all of this, however, they hit what they were after, causing 700 casualties of which 88 were killed. It took four days to clear the wreckage from the Vickers Factory and a number of days after that before full production was resumed.

However, as the Germans streaked for home additional RAF fighters were waiting for them and although the Messerschmitt 110 fighter-bombers returned unscathed, a total of seventeen Messerschmitt 110s failed to survive the day. The English countryside between Weybridge and Brighton was littered with burning or battered wrecks of Hermann Goering's favourite but inadequate fighter.

The only Bf 110 lost by ZG 2 on 4 September 1940 lies in a field near Shoreham; both crew were captured.

Another 4 September 1940 victim – M8+CP of 6/ZG 76 was seen to explode when attacked by Fg Off Ross Smither of 1 Sqn RCAF; both crew were killed. (Guschewski)

A pilot wounded in combat on 4 September 1940 was Hptm *Wilhelm Balthasar,* Gr Kdr *of III/JG 3.* (Morzinek)

5 September was a day of irritation for Fighter Command as, yet again, the *Luftwaffe* carried out a series of rolling attacks throughout the day against airfields in the south east. Bomber casualties were higher and the fighter-against-fighter combats vicious, as the following illustrates:

Pilot Officer Jan Zurakowski, 234 Squadron

I was diving from about 22,000ft to investigate two aircraft flying below when I noticed one Me 109 flying level and 'weaving'. I approached to about 150 yards and I fired about a two second burst. The Me 109 half rolled and dived close to the ground. At ground level and from thirty yards range, I opened fire until the guns stopped. Whilst firing, I had a problem in that due to the sudden descent to a low altitude, my front windscreen completely misted up and I was aiming using the wingtips of the Me 109 visible through the cockpit side panels. The Me 109 was flying very close to the ground but when some hills forced him a bit higher, I could see him better against the background of the sky so I started firing again until I ran out of ammunition and when I looked down, there was a town approaching. The Me 109 flew trailing smoke over Hastings, the canopy was jettisoned and the plane ditched about two miles from the shore and in a few minutes, the aircraft turned over and sank but the pilot was still in the water.

The misting up of Jan Zurakowski's cockpit which made it hard for him to see his victim also happened to his victim, so preventing the German pilot from seeing the approaching danger until too late:

Feldwebel Anton Ochsenkuehn, 9/JG 53

We took off from the airfield at Le Touquet at about 1500 hrs. Our task was a *Freie Jagd* in the London area. We were led by *Oblt* Jakob Stoll – I was *Rotte* Leader and, together with *Oblt* Herbert Seliger, we were flying the rear guard or *Deckungsrotte*.

As we were about to fly into the combat zone over the River Thames, we heard over the radio from our ground station, "Enemy planes over London." As far as I know, their altitude was given as 6,000m. Because we were nowhere near as high, we turned to the east and climbed to the necessary height. Then we changed our direction back to the combat zone. Very soon, we saw a Spitfire below us – *Oblt* Stoll attacked immediately and as far as I am aware, *Oblt* Josef Volk and *Uffz* Manfred Langer's attacks followed. However, all attacks were unsuccessful because the RAF pilot had seen us and was obviously proficient. Then I went over to attack, the Spitfire descended in a spin

Bf 109s of JG 53 at Le Touquet.
(Sauer)

and I stayed behind it without having the chance to shoot. After diving 2,000-3,000m, I was ordered to "break off pursuit and climb back up again." I let him know that I had understood and was about to climb back when my cockpit misted up so badly that I could not see a thing.

Now I did not want to put myself in danger of being surprised and shot down whilst in a slow climb so I put my nose down and waited until I had better visibility. I then looked back and I saw a plane behind me, far away and very small. I was not able to see if it was a friend or an enemy. Over the radio I tried to find out where my wingman was and the rest of the *Staffel*. I did not get a reply so I presumed that my radio was not working. So, for a while, we were flying one behind the other heading south but now I was having second thoughts. In this plane behind me there could be my wingman who in his efforts to catch up with me and looking too much in my direction could be surprised and shot down himself by an enemy fighter. Without hesitation, I turned and flew towards the plane but very quickly realised that it was a Spitfire which I recognised by the big radiator under its left wing. Instead of attacking, I turned back again hoping I could get away from the Spitfire but I was completely wrong. Because of the two turns, the Spitfire had got dangerously close to me so I flew at low level to get away. However, near the coast, I had to pull up over woodland and as this happened, I was hit in both radiators. The Messerschmitt slowed down alarmingly. I then flew over a town (probably Hastings) but over the water I had only an altitude of ten metres and an airspeed of 250kph. To be on the safe side, I threw off the canopy roof and, right after that, the engine

Anton Ochsenkuehn (far left) with Fw *Klapdohr,* Uffz *Kurt Sauer (POW 16 July 1941) and* Uffz *Anders.* (Volk)

broke down. I succeeded in ditching in such a way that I could get out
of the cockpit quickly; the Spitfire which had been playing a waiting
game and had followed me since the attack over the woodland circled
round me and then flew back towards England.

One pilot who, despite being taken prisoner on 5 September 1940, managed to escape back to Germany was Lt Franz von Werra of II/JG 3. Seen here after his return, he was killed in a flying accident in October 1941.

6 September would be similar to the day before with the Germans yet
again going after airfields and oil storage depots on the Thames in three
distinct phases. One German pilot was destined to be his *Geschwader*'s last
casualty before, to the RAF's relief, the Germans made a gross error by
changing tactics. No longer would airfields and aircraft manufacturers be
the sole objects of their attention:

Leutnant Max Himmelheber, *Gruppen Adjutant* I/JG 2

On the 6th, my *Geschwader* flew on a routine flight over southern
England. Until now, I had flown with *Stab*/JG 2 but today I was with
I/JG 2 under the command of *Hptm* Hennig Struempel. We flew up

to the southern outskirts of London and got involved in an air battle with British fighters. I received a hit in the radiator of my aircraft so that the engine was not able to work. I found myself at 10,000m and attempted to glide to one of our Red Cross boats in the Channel and then bale out. Approaching the coast, I flew over, at about 2,000m, a military airfield and was attacked by two Hurricanes which caused me to bale out. I landed in a meadow and as I was badly wounded, I was taken to a civilian hospital in the small town of Maidstone and there I was operated on. After a week, I was taken to a military hospital in Woolwich.

A Bf 109E of I/JG 2 over England. (Fiby)

Maj *Hennig Struempell (right) with* **Oblt** *Helmut Wick who was to replace him as Gr Kdr I/JG 2 on 7 September 1940.* (via Payne)

Another casualty on 6 September 1940 was this Bf 109E-4 of Uffz Hans Georg Schulte *of 7/JG 53.*

7 September 1940 dawned bright, clear and quiet – the RAF had no inkling at all that things were about to change. *Reichsmarschall* Goering had realised that the tactic of going for the fighter airfields was not having the desired result. He therefore decided that if the strategy changed to all-out attack on London, the RAF would commit every remaining fighter to the defence of the nation's capital. His belief was soon proved to be flawed.

There was little if no activity that morning and even then, the radar screens remained sinisterly clear until about 1600 hrs. The radars then picked up an ever increasing mass of enemy aircraft until in the region of 1,000 bombers and fighters clogged the screens, spread between altitudes of 14,000ft and 23,000ft. By 1630 hrs, more than twenty RAF fighter squadrons were either airborne or at readiness and the sight that greeted these RAF pilots must have been fearsome.

The RAF threw itself at the attackers but, against such odds, could do little to deter the Germans who, having dropped their bombs on London's dockland and setting much of it ablaze, turned for home. The attack had lasted just under an hour. However, the RAF succeeded in shooting down forty-one German aircraft that day, twenty-one of which were fighters that had tenaciously defended the bombers, allowing them to cause such devastation. Again, *Zerstoerers* were mauled, in this case ZG 2 who lost eight aircraft and were withdrawn from the battle some two days later. The RAF lost twenty-two fighters but only ten pilots lost their lives.

That night the *Luftwaffe* visited the capital again, causing more death and destruction. But it must be said that, sad as these deaths were, the change of tactic from bombing military targets to bombing those of a political, commercial and civilian nature gave Fighter Command the slight relief they needed. Although it was not obvious then, the Germans had as good as lost the Battle of Britain. However, there was no respite for either side's aircrew who would continue to fight and in some cases die over the remaining month and a half of the campaign.

8 September was very much an anti-climax. The fear that a German invasion fleet had set sail was unfounded and Fighter Command was allowed to send some of its squadrons away from the fighting for well earned rest and recovery. Only two small raids took place but they were heavily escorted by Messerschmitt 109s of JG 3, JG 26, JG 27 and JG 53, the latter *Geschwader* claiming the lion's share of the four RAF fighters lost that day. However, they lost three themselves – one in combat and two in an accident:

Oberleutnant **Heinz Wittmeyer,** *Stab* **I/JG 53**

I had belonged to JG 53 since August 1940 and, on 8 September, I was attached to *Stab* I/JG 53 being introduced into the work of an *Adjutant*. It was about my thirtieth operational flight. The order for that day was to fly close air support for a *Gruppe* of He 111s into the area east of London. We flew in a *Gruppe* formation at about 20,000ft.

Before crossing the line Dungeness–Hastings, I spotted three fighters north-north-west and reported this to the *Gruppen Kommandeur*. As a consequence of this, he gave the order to the *Gruppe* to turn towards them. At this time, the smallest RAF formation was three aircraft whereas we had the two or four aircraft *Rotte* or *Schwarm* so we thought that these aircraft were RAF. Very soon, the three were identified as Bf 109s – they had exactly the same altitude as ourselves and came straight towards us. Normally, they should have given way to us – Numbers One and Two did so and dropped their Bf 109s beneath our *Schwarm*. However, the third didn't. I tried at the very last second to avoid disaster by pushing my stick forward but it was, at least for the other pilot, too late. Both Bf 109s disintegrated and I found, without doing anything, that I was in open air.

A little later, I opened the parachute. I was more or less blind in my right eye (later, in a field hospital, a specialist took more than twenty metal splinters out of it). I could, however, see a bit with my left eye (six splinters). On that day, there was a strong wind from the north west. It blew me towards the French coast. When I touched the sea, I tried to free myself from the parachute, initially without success. This was good because the parachute became a kite and I became one of the first windsurfers! The kite brought me nearer to the coast but on becoming wetter, the parachute collapsed. This time I got free and swam for nearly an hour after which I was helped ashore by soldiers near Cap Gris-Nez.

The other pilot, unfortunately, did not get out of his Messerschmitt. I was later told that the *Staffel* to which the three Bf 109s that crossed our course belonged had been in a fight with Spitfires near London and the *Staffel* had broken up. They were on their way back to their airfield and the pilot who had collided with me was probably looking backwards to be sure that they were not attacked again. It seems that during the collision, a propeller blade cut the cockpit just before my head and the next blade behind my head cutting my seat belts. Beside my eyes, I was injured with a cut on my right shoulder.

I was told by fellow pilots visiting me in the hospital that the pilot who collided with me was a newcomer and had no experience[4]. I had to stay some months in hospital, returning to the *Ergaenzungsgruppe* of

Oblt *Heinz Wittmeyer (2nd from right) with, L to R,* Lt *Guenther Hess (2/JG 53),* Oblt *Hans Ohly (1/JG 53),* Hptm *Rolf Pingel (St Kap 2/JG 53) and* Hptm *Hans Karl Mayer (St Kap 1/JG 53).* (Schultz)

[4]This was *Oblt* Heinz Kunert, *Staffel Kapitaen* of 8/JG 53. He was not inexperienced and had nine air combat victories, his last being on 5 September 1940.

JG 53 in France and in Spring 1941 to I/JG 53 in Sicily. However, the eyesight of my right eye had not recovered enough (whereas the left eye was good again) and I had to stop flying as a fighter pilot and was posted to II *Fliegerkorps* in Sicily.

Officers of III/JG 53, early 1940 – few were to survive that year. Oblt Heinz Kunert is back row, 2nd from left. Others are: front row L to R Lt Josef Volk, 9/JG 53 (POW 11 November 1940), Oblt Heinz Wittenberg, Stab, Hptm Werner Moelders, Gr Kdr (+22 November 1941), Lt Walter Radlick, Adj (+2 October 1940), Lt Georg Claus, TO (+11 November 1940). Middle row L to R Oblt Otto Boenigk, St Kap 9/JG 53, Dr Soestmann, Oblt Wolf-Dietrich Wilcke, St Kap 7/JG 53 (+23 March 1944), Lt Hans Riegel, 7/JG 53 (+ 6 September 1940), Lt Jakob Stoll, 8/JG 53 (+ 17 September 1940), Lt Horst Von Wegeman (+ 9 March 1941). Back row L to R Lt Ernst Panten, Kunert, Lt Hans Fleitz, 8/JG 53 (+ 3 June 1940), Oblt Hans von Hahn, St Kap 8/JG 53.

The following day saw the *Luftwaffe* launch the start of co-ordinated day and night destruction of London in preparation for the start of Operation *SEELOEWE*, the German invasion of Great Britain. The orders to launch the invasion would be issued on 11 September and the Germans anticipated that the landing assault would take place on 21 September. Nevertheless, daylight operations on 9 September did not start until late in the afternoon when many bombers, heavily escorted, made for various targets in and around London. The German fighters were greatly committed, losing twelve Messerschmitt 109s and four 110s. Two of the Messerschmitt 109 pilots had very different experiences that day:

Oberleutnant Erwin Daig, 5/JG 27

The mission took place late in the afternoon. Our unit had been detailed to fly as escort to a formation of bombers which was attacking London Docks. We took off from Fiennes in the Pas de Calais and before we reached our destination, we encountered rather lively opposition from British fighters. In the course of this, my aircraft must have been hit as from then on I was unable to accelerate properly. When the German formation turned for France, I was unable to follow. At that time, I must have been the only German aircraft in the area. Then I made a mistake which was to cost me my freedom. Instead of going into a glide, assisted by my engine and trying to reach the French coast at high speed, I maintained my course and height (6,000-7,000m). Immediately, I was attacked by two British fighters which came from an easterly direction from above and turned in behind me. They fired and my aircraft was hit. I stood the aircraft 'on its head' and attempted to reach a layer of cloud which was covering the French coast and southern England at a height of about 2,000-3,000m. I felt that I was succeeding as I received no more hits but just before I reached cloud cover, I was fired at again and I now thought that I had another pursuer behind me. I then went into a dive and tried to reach the Channel by hedge-hopping. However, it was useless. The aircraft started to smoke and I was unable to see so I threw off the cabin roof. I was also losing speed. The last thing I saw was an area rising to the south with trees on top; in front of it was a large meadow covered in overturned lorries and other things to prevent gliders landing there. Then I must have hit the ground. That was it – the end of the chase, unfortunately!

Oblt *Erwin Daig.* (Daig)

Erwin Daig's fighter had been hit in the cooling system and he quickly jumped out of the plane, throwing down his gun and surrendering to troops from a nearby searchlight battery. This aircraft came in for close scrutiny by the RAF who noted that it carried a bomb rack. Although this was not the first time bomb racks had been discovered on Messerschmitt 109s, the full significance would not become clear until just under a month later when Messerschmitt 109s began to operate as *Jagdbombers* or *Jabos* – literally fighter-bombers.

Bf 109s of II/JG 27, early in the Battle of Britain. (via Moelders)

An unluckier pilot was *Feldwebel* Heinrich Hoehnisch of 1/JG 53. Now an experienced fighter pilot with six air combat victories, he had not increased his personal tally of kills since 13 August 1940. It was unlikely that he would shoot down anything else on 9 September – his unit had been 'chained' to the bomber formation and he was assigned to the lookout *Rotte:*

Feldwebel Heinrich Hoehnisch, 1/JG 53

On my last mission on 9 September 1940, our task was to give direct fighter cover to the rear of an He 111 bomber formation. One *Kette* of bombers got separated so our *Staffel* looked after them. We had only seven Bf 109s and I was the tail-end Charlie with *Ofw* Mueller.

Approaching London Docks, there was no contact with the enemy but I was sure that we could expect attacks out of the sun as soon as we turned 180 degrees for our return flight. To my surprise, I saw, when I was looking towards the rest of my *Staffel*, six Spitfires on a reciprocal course in a line about fifty metres above me. To avoid the inevitable attack, I tried to come up with my *Staffel* flying in front and below me. When I was level with my *Staffel Kapitaen*, I thought I had made it...

Heinrich Hoehnisch (left) just after he joined JG 53, early 1940. (Hoehnisch)

Combats on 9 September were confused. However, it would appear that the Duxford Wing, consisting of Spitfires of 19 Squadron and Hurricanes of 242 and 310 Squadrons were in the area south of London, close to Biggin Hill. 19 Squadron, led that day by Flt Lt Wilfrid Clouston, went after the fighters:

Flight Lieutenant Wilfrid Clouston, 19 Squadron

While on patrol leading the Squadron at 20,000ft, we encountered a large formation of enemy aircraft. We had been detailed by Wing Leader to attack fighters so I climbed and put the Squadron into position to attack seven Me 110s. Just as I was about to attack, two Me 109s crossed my sights so I turned on them. The rear one emitted glycol fumes after a short burst and then burst into flames. I then attacked the second Me 109 and fired the rest of the ammunition. I could see my shots hitting this aircraft and when my ammunition had finished, I saw him going down in a left hand gliding turn, looking rather the worse for wear...

Feldwebel Heinrich Hoehnisch

...There was a rattle like an explosion in my plane and, with the pressure of a blow torch, flames hit my face. With greatest difficulty, I got out of the plane. I landed with severe burns to my face and bullet wounds to my right calf. I stayed in hospital in Woolwich for two months.

September 1940

THIS AND NEXT PAGE
Drawn by Heinrich Hoehnisch after his capture;
his sketches vividly portray his last flight.

9. September 1940

9. September 1940

Heinrich Hoehnisch was quickly captured, his aircraft crashing close to the fighter base at Biggin Hill. Interrogated by RAF officers and still in great pain from his burns, he gave away no information on his unit. In fact, he boasted that he knew all about the RAF airfields because British prisoners of war "gave away such a lot of information of this sort when interrogated." What particularly interested the RAF was found in the remains of his fighter. On the underside of one of the wings, towards the trailing edge, were two small discs about the size of a penny, painted like the RAF roundel with the date '13.8.40'. Today, Heinrich Hoehnisch can explain this unusual marking:

Feldwebel Heinrich Hoehnisch

On 13 August 1940, we had an escort mission for some Ju 88s near Portsmouth. I shared the shooting down of three Hurricanes flying in line. After that, we had a dogfight above a circling Bf 110 *Gruppe*. I hit a Spitfire between the fuselage and the wing with two 20mm shells. I was then hit in my right wing by a Hurricane which came up behind me. I escaped by rolling and diving. The Hurricane followed to sea-level but turned away when I climbed for home.

The days that followed 9 September were relatively quiet for the German fighter pilots. 10 September saw the return of bad weather and a corresponding reduction in German sorties. Bad weather again on 11 September prevented operations until mid-afternoon and then, because of apparent faulty routing for the bombers, the majority of the escorting Messerschmitt 109s returned early leaving much for the Messerschmitt 110s to do. Messerschmitt 109 losses were light – only three were lost in combat – but the Messerschmitt 110s lost seven in the attack on London and whilst escorting a smaller attack on Southampton by *Erprobungsgruppe* 210. Although the RAF wreaked havoc on the Heinkel 111s attacking London, thirty of their fighters were lost that day and eleven pilots were killed. Even two fighter Bristol Blenheims of 235 Squadron were lost escorting Fleet Air Arm aircraft attacking the German invasion barges. All in all, the Germans fared better that day and it was a relief to the RAF that the next two days saw the return, yet again, of bad weather which allowed the RAF light bombers to go on the offensive. Such daylight attacks were not without incident. For example, at 1545 hrs on 12 September, three Bristol Blenheims from Coastal Command's 59 Squadron took off to attack shipping off Le Havre. They picked up an escort of three Blenheims from 235 Squadron and then attacked a convoy, failing to hit a single ship, before a lone Messerschmitt 109 intervened:

Leutnant Alfred Zeis, 1/JG 53

I had been on a ferry flight from Rennes to Le Touquet and was flying along the coast. The weather was bad with almost total low-lying cloud cover. Just before I reached Le Havre, I saw some fountains on the edge of the harbour basin and saw three planes heading for the clouds, one after the other. At full throttle, I tried to intercept before they could reach the cloud and just before the last one disappeared, I expended all my 20mm ammunition against him without success – the range was too great. I followed the last plane into cloud, flying on instruments, and came up behind three Blenheims flying close together. I first shot at the engines of the left-hand Blenheim and then attacked the right one before they disappeared into cloud but not before my Messerschmitt had received some hits. Before they disappeared, I saw some effects of my fire – black smoke coming out of one plane. By now, I had to turn back and, using my compass, flew in the direction of Le Havre between two layers of cloud. Suddenly, another *Kette* of three Blenheims appeared in front of me – they climbed and fired at me. I was then hit again and it was high time I reached Le Havre airfield. When I arrived, the visibility was very poor and my plane totally covered in oil. Fortunately, I could land but the engine had to be changed and other repairs carried out. Two days later, I flew back to join the rest of the *Staffel*.

In my combat report, I said that at least one Blenheim had been damaged and when I was asked, I did not completely rule out a kill. However, it is probable that none of the Blenheims received severe damage because I did not have any cannon ammunition left. A victory was therefore questionable.

Lt *Alfred Zeis*. (Schultz)

Alfred Zeis's normal Bf 109 with his tenth victory tab, the Blenheim on 12 September 1940, visible on the rudder. (Sauer)

Unusually for the Germans, despite there being no positive evidence of a kill, Alfred Zeis was allowed to claim a Blenheim as his tenth kill. The 235 Squadron diary disagrees:

235 Squadron Diary Entry, 12 September 1940

Plt Off Wordsworth, Sgt Sutton and Flt Sgt Nelson provided bomber escort for three bomber aircraft to Le Havre. Four Me 109s were sighted. One attacked bombers but was driven off by Blenheims. Rear gunners concentrated fire on this aircraft and [it was] believed damaged.

Unusually, no record was made of the damage to Alfred Zeis's Messerschmitt 109.

Friday 13 September was again a quiet day for both sides whilst operations on the following day, again being hampered by bad weather, were restricted to a few small bombing attacks using clouds as cover. Unfortunately for Fighter Command, towards the end of the day the weather improved allowing many of the *Jagdgeschwader* to undertake *Freie Jagd* over much of southern England with some success, claiming twenty-five RAF fighters and allowing the German top scorers to increase their personal tallies. *Maj* Werner Moelders of JG 51 claimed his thirty-seventh kill, *Hptm* Adolf Galland of JG 26 his thirty-second, *Oblt* Joachim Muenchberg of 7/JG 26 his twentieth and *Hptm* Rolf Pingel of I/JG 26 his fifteenth. Twelve RAF fighters were lost in action and the RAF claimed to have shot down sixteen German aircraft. In reality, only three fighters and three bombers were lost that day.

If the results on 14 September left the RAF downbeat, the reduced attacks since the change in tactics on 7 September, particularly the German penchant for rolling attacks, had given Fighter Command a well needed breathing space. The attrition the RAF had suffered up to that date would, if it had continued, have seen Fighter Command on its knees prior to what the *Luftwaffe* was going to throw at them exactly half way through the month. However, with their backs against the wall, invasion imminent and with nothing else to lose, the RAF's fighter pilots were, surprisingly, relatively rested and in high spirits. The opposite could be said of the German bomber and fighter aircrew, some of whom had been in almost constant action since the start of the war. Despite all that they had done, there seemed to be no reduction in the numbers of Spitfires and Hurricanes that

Hptm *Rolf Pingel of I/JG 26; the award of his Ritterkreuz was promulgated on 14 September 1940.* (Pingel)

they kept on meeting over the skies of southern England. However, as a means of emasculating Fighter Command in order to carry out the invasion, the Germans had been planning an all out attack on the British capital and on Sunday 15 September, they decided to do just that.

The first attack was picked up on radar just after 1100 hrs as the Dornier 17s of KG 76 formed up just south of Calais. At the same time, Messerschmitt 109s of II/LG 2 carried out what was a relatively new concept – that of Messerschmitt 109s carrying bombs, much like the Messerschmitt 110s of *Erprobungsgruppe* 210. They attacked railway targets in south-eastern London but what they did was not regarded by the British as fair as one participating Austrian pilot recalls:

Oberleutnant **Viktor Krafft,** *Kompaniechef Stab* **II/LG 2**

A British newspaper wrote when our *Gruppe* flew for the first time over Kent: 'Today flew a group of German fighters over Kent and London. Nobody had expected they were carrying bombs but they did so. It is not fair to fly like a fighter and then to drop bombs like a bomber.' I should say that we didn't do it because we were unfair. It was just a new development as is usual in war.

The unfair weapon – a 250kg bomb underneath a Bf 109. (Sauer)

However, it was the unfortunate Dornier 17s that suffered in that first attack. Spitfires went after the fighters whilst the bombers were initially engaged by the Hurricanes, attacking with such ferocity that the formation split up making it hard for the fighter escort to protect them. Later, Sqn Ldr Douglas Bader led his Duxford Wing consisting of two Spitfire and three Hurricane squadrons into the fray with the end result that, for once, the Germans were outnumbered and what followed was inevitable. One German pilot, *Oblt* Erwin Moll of 3/KG 76, later felt obliged to write alongside his logbook entry for that day, "Target London. Very heavy fighter defence" – the first and only time he had ever felt a need to write such a comment.

Even though the German bombers reached their intended target of the railway lines at Latchmere Junction, damage was slight but then the RAF fighters began to take their toll as the Dornier 17s headed back towards the safety of the Messerschmitt 109 escort in the Maidstone area. However, the German fighters were having their own problems:

Feldwebel Herbert Tzschoppe, 1/JG 53

On 15 September 1940 I, with *Uffz* Kopperschlaeger, was one of the last of the *Staffel* to take off – we had to fly as the *Deckungsrotte*. We flew at the back of the escort formation.

The *Staffel Kapitaen*, *Oblt* Ohly had to turn back with radio trouble and the lead was given to *Ofw* Mueller. We were flying at about 3,500m and had to fly with our flaps down so that we could stay close to the slower bombers. During a turn, we were attacked by Spitfires coming out of the sun – Mueller was hit in the arm and broke away and my plane was hit in both wings. I wanted to get back to France, thinking of my fiancée and forthcoming wedding at the end of September, and tried to hide in the clouds which were at about 1,500m. However, when I came out of the clouds, I was hit by a second burst so I threw off the cabin roof and undid my seat belt. I now think that the drills I learned in flying training then saved my life (we were often woken up at night and had to say what to do if we were hit – throw off the cabin roof, undo the seat belts, jump out and pull the rip cords). A third burst hit home – from the instrument panel there came flames like an oxyacetylene torch and my hands and face were severely burned. An explosion followed and I found myself hanging on a parachute…

Fw *Herbert Tzschoppe (2nd from left) with, L to R:* Uffz *Ghesla (POW 5 October 1940), Tzschoppe, Fw Hoehnisch (POW 9 September 1940), Lt Zeis (POW 5 October 1940), Oblt Ohly, Hptm Mayer (+ 17 October 1940), Lt Schultz,* Uffz *Karl (POW 2 September 1940) and Uffz Ruehl (+ 4 June 1941).*

Pilot Officer Tony Lovell, 'B' Flight, 41 Squadron

Flying as Blue Two, [we] broke up to attack Me 109s which were attacking us. [I] sighted my Me 109 turning east and diving. I dived after him and chased him for some fifteen miles in and out of cloud. After first burst, white fumes came from his port wing root but he carried on. I gave him two more bursts and he caught fire and I saw him bale out and being attended to on the ground.

Pilots of 41 Sqn prior to the Summer of 1940 – Plt Off Tony Lovell is in the middle row 3rd from right. (Shipman)

John Sampson

I was eighteen years of age and resident in Adisham near Canterbury in September 1940. On the morning of Sunday 15 September, a friend (the son of the local gamekeeper) and I were out shooting in the woods. We heard the sound of aerial combat and then saw someone descending by parachute. The pilot (I now know to be Tzschoppe) came to earth at the edge of a wood near to where we were standing. He surrendered to us (we both had 12-bore shotguns) and unloaded his pistol and handed it to us. We handed him over to a detachment of New Zealand soldiers who quickly appeared on the scene – this would have been about two to three miles from where the Me 109 crashed at Adisham Court. The victorious Spitfire overflew us after we had apprehended the German pilot.

Feldwebel **Herbert Tzschoppe**

…Two Spitfires circled me at full bank – the first pilot saluted and I did the same. I came down in a mixed forest and got hung up in a tree about five feet from the ground. I released myself from the parachute and landed heavily, hurting my knees. Two youths and shortly after that soldiers appeared and I was taken prisoner. I was taken by ambulance to a hospital where my burns were treated very well. The nursing was excellent, especially by the Irish nurses who I can remember very well! I was then taken to the Royal Herbert Hospital in London where I met *Ofw* Mueller and three other pilots from my *Staffel* who had been shot down before me.

It was a particularly bad mission for I/JG 53 who lost four more pilots, including two *Staffel Kapitaene*. The whole *Geschwader* claimed fourteen RAF fighters as means of retribution. It is thought that at least Messerschmitt Bf 109s were lost in the first major action of the day and if the *Jagdgeschwader* thought that they were in for a rest, they were gravely mistaken.

The two I/JG 53 Staffel Kapitaen *lost in the first attack on 15 September 1940:* Oblt *Rudi Schmidt of 2/JG 53 (centre) with (left)* Lt *Guenther Hess and (right)* Lt *Gebhardt Dittmar (+ 6 September 1940)…* (Schultz)

...and Oblt *Julius Haase* of 3/JG 53 *(second from right) with (L to R),* Uffz *Karl Kuhl,* Oblt *Wolfgang Lippert (+13 December 1941),* Ofw *Erich Kuhlmann (+ 2 September 1940).* (Rupp)

The pilots of JG 53 had barely enough time to land, refuel and rearm before they were sent off again; this was typical of many other *Jagdgeschwader* who were involved in the first attack of the day. This time the targets were the Royal Victoria, West India and Surrey Commercial Docks in eastern London and the attacking force was even bigger, made up of 114 Dornier 17s and Heinkel 111s flying in three parallel columns, three miles apart, the whole formation being some thirty miles wide.

Buzzing around all sides of this monstrous formation were the fighters including, on this occasion, Messerschmitt 110s from V(Z)/LG 1 and I/ZG 26. The RAF threw at least twenty-nine Spitfire and Hurricane squadrons at the formation coming from as far as Middle Wallop to the west and Duxford to the north. The RAF fighter pilots were tenacious, flying and fighting as if their lives depended on it. For some, this was not enough to ensure their survival:

Unteroffizier Heinrich Ruehl, 1/JG 53

We were flying in a *Schwarm* led by *Oblt* Ohly. I was his *Rottenflieger*. We were escorting a formation of Do 17s. Short of London, the bomber formation was suddenly attacked from the front by two enemy squadrons. The front-most squadron attacked through the bomber formation and pulled up. *Oblt* Ohly attacked the rearmost squadron. During this, I saw a Spitfire [sic] which flew through the bomber formation pulled up and turned. At this moment, I took aim and opened fire and saw in between the wing and fuselage a tongue of flame shoot out.

The fighter immediately caught fire and dived into the increasing cloud and, although the crash was not observed, both he and *Uffz* Kopperschlaeger were each credited with a Spitfire. It is likely that they had pounced on the Hurricanes of 303 Squadron which lost two aircraft – one pilot baling out, the other never to be seen again.

A Bf 109E of I/JG 53 is prepared for the next sortie. (Sauer)

As well as inflicting mortal damage on some of the bombers, the RAF succeeded in shooting down at least nine Messerschmitt 109s and three 110s of V(Z)/LG 1. Most of the aircrew shot down were not as fortunate as the two Messerschmitt 109s lost by I/LG 2 that afternoon. *Uffz* Herbert Streibing was shot down by one of the 303 Squadron Hurricanes that managed to avoid the attention of 1/JG 53, the German pilot crash-landing in Essex. The other LG 2 pilot had a similar experience:

Unteroffizier **August Klik, 2/LG 2**

Our operational airfield was Calais Marck on the Channel coast. The task of our *Staffel* was escorting bombers to England. Our losses were always very high because we flew on the furthest flank of the escort and so had no rear cover. Because of that, we were often pushed away to the east when attacked by British fighters so a fair number of pilots had to ditch because of lack of fuel and some of them drowned.

On 15 September, our order was: Victoria Docks, London; escort for I/KG 1, 5/KG 2, 6/KG 26 and KG 53. We were told good weather and not much opposition. However, things were very different.

Before we reached Tonbridge, heavy AA fire welcomed us and the sky began to cloud over (seven tenths cloud cover). Suddenly, the sky was full of British fighters. The first group of bombers was torn apart and disappeared into a protective cloud bank. During the subsequent air battle, we were pushed away to the east – again! The variable amounts of cloud and the tumult of battle made it difficult to tell the difference between friend and foe.

The cloud cover then broke up and just in front of me, a Hurricane approached from the right, in a steep turn. It was fifty metres and firing a broadside – nothing could go wrong for me! I was therefore so surprised that I made the mistake – like a beginner. I put my aircraft into a steep climb to see if my burst had hit home when there were hits in my starboard wing. Two planes were heading straight for me but the hits in my plane's wing must have come from another plane from behind and the left because the two aircraft did not show any muzzle flashes (perhaps they were as surprised as I was!).

500m below me on my right, there was a long cloud bank. It was the only protection against half a dozen British fighters...

August Klik (3rd from right) and other prisoners seen in Canada later in the war.

Flying Officer Leonard Haines, 19 Squadron

Whilst leading Green Section on a patrol south of London, I noticed AA fire just west of London and, on investigating, I noticed a force of some forty enemy aircraft which I could not identify. I put my section into line astern and made for the AA fire when two Me 109s appeared to my right. I accordingly turned and attacked them. I gave one a burst (deflection from above) and it half-rolled and dived vertically to 12,000ft where it straightened out. I had dived after it and as it finished its dive, I recommenced my attack. I was going faster than the enemy aircraft and I continued firing until I had to pull away to avoid collision. The enemy aircraft half-rolled and dived vertically with black smoke coming from underneath the pilot's seat, it seemed. I followed it down until it entered cloud at 6,000ft...

Unteroffizier August Klik

...I considered what had happened. All instruments showed normal readings, only the radiator temperature gauge was alarmingly high. It was getting hot in the cockpit and when I tried to put the safety pin of the cockpit hood into its second notch, the hood suddenly flew off.

The cloud bank had come to an end and below me there was the Thames Estuary. Because of the air combats around Maidstone and the bomber group having been pushed away, much fuel had been consumed – the red fuel warning lamp began to flicker.

There were three alternatives to be considered: baling out, a forced landing or the vague possibility of flying out to sea and being fished out by a German air sea rescue aircraft. Point number three was not worth the risk; point number one only in an emergency as a few days earlier we had been warned not to bale out as Polish pilots shot at every parachute over the coastal area! The engine was at only 880rpm so I turned towards dry land and made a smooth landing on an island in the Thames Estuary.

After five minutes, some Home Guards came and took away my sunglasses, watch and pistol. In return for these, they offered me a bottle of beer! I was taken to a cell in a fort at Sheerness by an army jeep and, together with some other prisoners, we went to Chatham. Later than evening, we were taken to a building in Hyde Park for interrogation. Just at this moment, London was receiving another bombing raid...

The cloud, a saviour for August Klik, was also a saviour for the intended targets that late Sunday afternoon. Another bomber formation arrived over London only to find their targets obscured by cloud and, in frustration, their

THIS AND NEXT PAGE
August Klik's Bf 109 comes in for some attention after it had been taken away to be recycled. (Cornwell)

bombs were dropped on the south-eastern outskirts of the capital as they turned for home, still being attacked mercilessly by the RAF fighters.

As the massive phalanx of German aircraft headed for home, another raid was developing to the west when unescorted Heinkel 111s attacked Portland and then, two hours later, the hard-worked *Erprobungsgruppe* 210 attacked the Supermarine Factory at Southampton. Both raids were ineffective (although the former raid lost one bomber) and it was left to the nocturnal German bombers to attack London, one of the six attacks before midnight being experienced first hand by August Klik.

The *Luftwaffe* had flown in excess of 1,000 sorties on that Sunday, losing fifty-six aircraft which in human terms was eighty-one aircrew killed or missing, sixty-three taken prisoner and thirty-one wounded. The cost in terms of fighters was three Messerschmitt 110s and six crew killed, twenty-three Messerschmitt 109s and nine pilots killed, eleven prisoners and two wounded. Twenty-eight RAF fighters were lost, twelve pilots killed, twelve wounded and, unusually, one prisoner (Sgt John Potter of 19 Squadron – a victim of JG 26). The Germans succeeded in causing damage to the railway lines (but rail traffic was only disrupted for three days) whilst the Docks had got away unscathed. Therefore, the day for the Germans was a failure – their bombers had not succeeded in any of their aims, the fighters, despite carrying out close escort, had failed to protect their charges and, notwithstanding all the German efforts, the RAF was still a potent force. Adding the cost in human terms and aircraft lost, it was a bitter pill for the German aircrew to swallow and as such, must have been their nadir. Now we recognise that it was the turning point in the Battle of Britain, although neither side had realised this yet.

Bad weather helped give both sides a rest on 16 September. A bomber formation turned back because of the conditions. The escort from JG 51, however, continued and although *Maj* Moelders claimed his thirty-eighth kill and *Oblt* Claus his thirteenth, the only unlucky victim was Plt Off Edward Watson of 605 Squadron who, wounded, managed to crash-land his Hurricane at Detling in Kent. 17 September saw the German bomber crews taking another day's rest, leaving the fighters, no longer chained to the bombers, to carry out a series of aggressive *Freie Jagd* in the evening. Three Messerschmitt 109s were lost and their pilots killed as opposed to four Hurricanes and two pilots.

18 September was a busier day with an early morning *Freie Jagd*, followed by an escorted bomber attack and then a lightly escorted bomber attack on oil installations at Gravesend. Fighter Command responded to each raid correctly – leaving the *Freie Jagd*, sending an adequate response to the escorted raid and then shooting down nine bombers in the last raid of the day, including one of the German fighters carrying out a simultaneous *Freie Jagd*:

Leutnant **Erich Bodendiek,** *Gruppen Technischer Offizier,* **II/JG 53**

I remember that the dogfight took place somewhere in the region of Tonbridge at 8,000m and happened on a remarkable afternoon. After three missions that day, those planes which were still serviceable, about eighteen in all, took off on a *Freie Jagd*. I was not flying my usual plane but, as I was the *Technischer Offizier*, I had to fly a plane with a new automatic propeller just to test it. That was my bad luck, having that bloody plane on that day for the first time because that 'automatic thing' turned the angle of the propeller so that an average speed was always maintained and not a kmh more! That meant trouble when starting and trouble at high altitude as the plane was nearly always unmanoeuvrable and swaggered through the air like a pregnant duck.

It was fine weather with clouds at an altitude of about 8,300m and out of this swung the RAF fighters when we were at 8,000m. They were obviously directed by radar but just missed us as they came out of clouds about a kilometre to the right of us. The *Gruppen Kommandeur*, *Hptm* von Maltzahn, did the best he could by climbing and trying to hide in the clouds. Everybody succeeded but me, thanks to my excellent propeller. My aircraft could not climb like the others had and therefore all the RAF fighters turned on me and I had no chance of escaping by diving as that wonderful propeller would ensure that I would travel at just 300 to 350kmh. Therefore I decided to fly straight ahead trying to gain altitude a metre at a time, perhaps reaching cloud without being shot down. I saw the Spitfires flying around me and shooting and my plane was hit several times. I heard the bullets hitting the armoured plate behind me but I was not hurt. Finally, one of them dived down, gaining speed and pulled up vertically and shot exactly when I flew over him. He then hit my fuel tank which caught fire immediately. Within a second, my cabin was full of smoke and fire and I had to get out…

Lt *Erich Bodendiek, October 1939.* (Bodendiek)

Pilot Officer Bobby Oxspring, 66 Squadron

It appears that we had three patrols that day but it was only on the last one that we had a fight. It appears that we intercepted some Ju 88s with Me 109s covering, near Dover. I clobbered one which appeared to catch fire and the pilot baled out. My combat report says this happened a few miles north of Dover. I then fired at another from which I and my Number Two saw pieces fall off but in the ensuing melee, we didn't know the result and I claimed a damaged.

This all occurred over east Kent between 30,000ft and 20,000ft and the time was approximately 1700 hrs. The log also records that there was thick haze from 19,000ft to ground level and heavy cirrus around 30,000ft. So it was difficult to see any resulting crash either on the ground or in the Channel. We were accompanied by 92 Squadron that day and, as I say, the air was thick with aircraft. I, for one, never saw the Ju 88s for certain but from the initial contact, I was certainly concerned with the Me 109s in the same area.

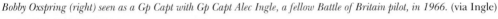

Bobby Oxspring (right) seen as a Gp Capt with Gp Capt Alec Ingle, a fellow Battle of Britain pilot, in 1966. (via Ingle)

Leutnant Erich Bodendiek

...I managed to get out and opened my parachute very quickly because I knew that there were high winds at that altitude and I calculated that it would take me thirty minutes or so to reach land. In the meantime, I would have covered nearly fifty kilometres and with the Channel being thirty-five kilometres wide, perhaps I had a chance to cross it!

Unfortunately, or should I say my good luck, the wind blew me the wrong direction so that I was driven along the coast and I finally dropped in the sea about two miles off Folkestone. I was collected by the Coastguards and overnight I was the guest of the Royal Artillery in Folkestone. They were rather suspicious because I did not wear a normal uniform, only breeches and white socks (I lost my fur-lined boots in the air) and a white pullover. I also had no identification, only my Iron Cross First Class which I had been awarded that afternoon and which I had put in my pocket. In my pocket, they also found some British money – the remains of the pounds I had when we were stationed on Guernsey. They must have thought I was a spy and must have been happy to hand me over to the RAF the next day. I was then taken to London – there they knew everything about me and my unit.

The final twelve days of September were to prove to be an anticlimax for both sides. On 19 September, Adolf Hitler postponed Operation *SEELOEWE* and the *Luftwaffe* began to change its tactics again, switching the emphasis of bombing attacks on London from day to night and increasing the use of Messerschmitt 109 *Jabo*s. In addition to those units already designated for such attacks, each *Jagdgeschwader* had to designate one *Staffel* in each *Gruppe* as the *Jabostaffel*, a decision not at all popular with the pilots:

Gefreiter Heinz Zag, 8/JG 53

I had joined 8/JG 53 in early September 1940, expecting to be a fighter pilot. I flew one of the first Bf 109s in the *Staffel* which was modified to carry a bomb. However, the *Staffel* was not properly trained, which concerned me, I did not think it was a good idea – we had a short enough flying range before being weighed down by a bomb!

In twelve days time, Heinz Zag would experience the limitations of his *Staffel* and his Messerschmitt 109 *Jabo* first hand. In the mean time, *Jabo* training for the designated *Staffeln* increased, probably as a result of the success of the *Jabo* attack on London on 20 September which achieved its aim. Just one of the escorting fighters was lost whilst the RAF fighters, scrambled to intercept the *Jabo*s too late, lost seven fighters to JG 2 and JG 26. Such an error on the part of the controllers would not be repeated.

The Jabo Staffel *of I/JG 53 – 3 Staffel. L to R:* Gefr *Felix Sauer,* Uffz *Alexander Bleymueller (+ 14 May 1943),* Fhr *Walter Seiz,* Gefr *Alfred Baumer,* Oblt *Walter Rupp,* St Kap *(POW 17 October 1940). Front:* Lt *Wolfgang Tonne,* Lt *Karl Leonhard.* (Sauer)

Trying to emulate the success of 21 September, the Germans attempted the same tactic as the day before but the RAF was wise. Only *Maj* Adolf Galland managed to shoot at one of the RAF fighters – Plt Off Thomas Sherrington of 92 Squadron managing to force-land his damaged Spitfire successfully. Operations on the days that followed were similar if not sporadic but 23 September saw a sharp increase in combats and losses – eleven RAF fighters for the same number of Messerschmitt 109s. One of the losses was one twenty year-old *Faehnrich* Hans-Joachim Marseille of 1/LG 2 who managed to ditch in the Channel and was rescued; he would shoot down his seventh victim on 27 September before transferring to 4/JG 52 and then 3/JG 27. He would be dead in exactly two years and one week after his ditching but not before he had shot down a total of 158 aircraft.

Preparing to load a 250 kg bomb to a Bf 109E-4/B. (Sauer)

The only JG 2 pilot to claim a victory on 20 September 1940 was Oblt *Hans Hahn (left),* St Kap *of 4/JG 2 seen here with* Lt *Julius Meimberg.* (Morzinek)

24 September would have been another day of sporadic activity if it were not for two incidents. *Erprobungsgruppe* 210 carried out a lightning fast attack on the Supermarine works at Southampton, losing just one of their number to AA fire. Although production was not affected, forty-two workers were killed. Another attack later that afternoon was similarly unsuccessful but this time, two of the Messerschmitt 110 escorts were shot down. The second incident occurred a little earlier:

Major **Adolf Galland**, *Geschwader Kommodore* **JG 26**

After a bombing raid on London, I attacked approximately thirty British fighters in the area of Southend but then got bounced during the approach by another squadron. The British formation broke up and then I attacked a single Hurricane which was at a higher altitude (about fifty metres) from behind climbing up and from sixty metres, and I saw it burst into flames. Thereupon, I saw the pilot bale out.

Fg Off Harold Bird-Wilson of 17 Squadron was Galland's fortieth kill for which Galland was awarded the Oakleaves to the Knight's Cross. Galland's 'rival', *Maj* Werner Moelders had achieved his fortieth kill on 20 September.

Maj *Werner Moelders in the cockpit of a Bf 109F. He first flew this variant operationally on 9 October 1940.*

The remainder of the month saw a series of attacks occurring to the west with the Bristol Aeroplane Company factory at Filton near Bristol being attacked on the 25th and the Supermarine factory, again, on 26 September. In the former attack, the RAF controllers got it wrong and misread the German intentions. The result was that the bombers reached their target almost unopposed, carpet bombing Filton. Ninety people were killed or fatally wounded and over 150 injured but the factory was not completely destroyed and full production was resumed a few months later. For the first time in a number of weeks, the escort was made up from Messerschmitt 110s of ZG 26 as well as Messerschmitt 109s from I and II/JG 2 and 5/JG 53. The twin-engined fighters did well and lost just three aircraft from III *Gruppe* and just two crew (one being taken prisoner and the other killed). The attack on the Supermarine factory the following day was also escorted by ZG 26 and, again, the attack was successful – only one bomber and two Messerschmitt 110s were lost and the factory was so badly damaged that construction of the Spitfire was dispersed away from Southampton.

However, perhaps the *Luftwaffe* had taken heart at these two successes and the appearance of the Messerschmitt 110 becoming effective again. 27 September was to prove them wrong and the death knell of the Messerschmitt 110 as a day fighter was sounded.

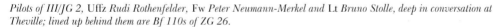

Pilots of III/JG 2, Uffz *Rudi Rothenfelder,* Fw *Peter Neumann-Merkel and* Lt *Bruno Stolle, deep in conversation at Theville; lined up behind them are Bf 110s of ZG 26.*

The day started with the old tactic of rolling attacks – the first clash occurring at 1000 hrs. Ten Messerschmitt 110s of what was left of V(Z)/LG 1 and thirteen Messerschmitt 110s of II and III/ZG 76 were tasked as an escort for Junkers 88s of I/KG 77. Messerschmitt 109 escort was undertaken by a number of units. The RAF was ready for all of them and ripped into the formation. Three Junkers 88s were lost as were eight of the escorting Messerschmitt 110s. V(Z)/LG 1 lost seven of their eleven aircraft including the *Gruppen* Kommandeur, *Hptm* Horst Liensberger and the *Staffel Kapitaen* of 15(Z)/LG 1, *Oblt* Ulrich Freiherr von Gravenreuth. With eleven aircrew dead and three prisoner, following their return to France the *Gruppe* was disbanded and its survivors withdrawn to southern Germany where they formed the nucleus of I/NJG 3. Only by making a break for home when the sky appeared to be clear of RAF fighters were twelve of the thirteen ZG 76 crews saved. The pilot of their only casualty was lucky to survive:

Hptm *Horst Liensberger*, Gr Kdr *of V(Z)/LG 1, killed in action 27 September 1940*. (Eimannsberger)

Oberleutnant Wilfried von Eichborn, *Geschwaderadjutant* ZG 76

27 September 1940 was an attack on an airfield north of London [sic]. Our *Geschwader* only had a third of its strength available and was quickly engaged by British fighters; we lost half of our number, the rest escaped to France. With one of my engines hit, I had to try to reach the

Bf 110s of 5/ZG 26. (D'Elsa)

The wing of Hptm *Liensberger's Bf 110 coded L1+XB frames the orchestra – he was to meet his death in this aircraft.* (Eichhorn)

coast by diving. I stupidly hoped to avoid more attacks but the British fighters followed me to the Channel, then a cable fire broke out in the fuselage and the aircraft burst into flames. With burns on my hands and to my head, I succeeded in setting down on the relatively calm sea and jumped into the water. However, my *Bordfunker* had baled out at high speed and was killed when he hit the sea. After drifting towards the Atlantic for several hours, kept afloat by my life jacket, later that afternoon I was picked up by a fishing boat and landed at Hastings. After a short time in a field hospital near Sevenoaks, I was brought to the Royal Herbert Hospital in Woolwich where I was put into a room with thirty German officers. I heard my neighbour in the next bed say to his neighbour the other side after looking at me, "Will that ever be a face again?" It did, the doctors attributing it to the long bath in sea water. The only annoying thing was that at Sevenoaks they had wrapped my face in cotton wool which now had to be laboriously picked off!

As this battered formation retreated, another raid, further to the west, would also see a further unit being decimated and, yet again, the losses would be just Messerschmitt 110s. It was *Erprobungsgruppe* 210's task to attack the Parnall Aircraft Factory at Yate near Bristol. Escort was provided by ZG 26 with elements of JG 2 and JG 53 covering the route to the coast and the return. This time a single unit, 504 Squadron, attacked the formation head-on, causing it to veer away, jettison its bombs and run for home. It was then that four more RAF fighter squadrons ripped into the

2nd from the left facing camera is Oblt Arthur Niebuhr. *He was transferred from 5/ZG 26 to be* St Kap *of 4/ZG 26 and was killed over Dorset on 27 September.* (D'Elsa)

survivors, chasing them back across the Channel. Six Messerschmitt 110s from ZG 26 were lost, including a *Staffel Kapitaen* and a *Gruppenadjutant*, whilst *Erprobungsgruppe* 210 lost four, including a very experienced *Gruppen Kommandeur* and *Staffel Kapitaen*, both of whom would be posthumously awarded the Knight's Cross.

The net result of these two attacks was that, apart from one more day in the Battle of Britain, Messerschmitt 110s were never seen in any great numbers. The reputation and effectiveness of the *Luftwaffe's* much vaunted 'Destroyer' had been well and truly destroyed. Furthermore, both attacks had been thwarted with the Germans suffering heavy losses.

As the second major offensive of the day was still fighting its way back home, the *Luftwaffe* switched back to attacking London, using Junkers 88s of KG 77 and Heinkel 111s of KG 53 in a series of rolling attacks interspersed with *Freie Jagd*. The day would be hard work for the German fighter pilots as the logbook of *Oblt* Jochen Schypek of 5/JG 54 shows – firstly escorting the early morning attack on London, then escorting Heinkel 111s attacking the same target around midday followed by another escort mission to London in the late afternoon. In between the second and third operational flight, he also had to test fly another Messerschmitt 109, presumably so that it could be flown by another pilot later that afternoon. However, the cost to the Germans was eighteen fighters shot down or written off and even KG 77 lost eight of their number during the first afternoon attack in addition to the three lost that morning. RAF losses in action were a total of twenty-nine but, as high as they might seem, the *Luftwaffe's* losses and continued failures were much worse and harder to bear.

Hptm *Helmut Wick*, Gr Kdr *of I/JG 2 got his thirty-third and thirty-fourth kills on 30 September 1940.* (Morzinek)

The next two days were quieter, albeit German fighters managed to account for seventeen RAF fighters on 28 September for the loss of just two fighters in combat, proving that despite what the RAF thought, the Messerschmitt 109s could still teach the Spitfires and Hurricanes a lesson. However, the last lesson of the month for both sides, and what would later prove to be the last major daylight attack during the Battle of Britain, occurred on 30 September.

Throughout the day, the *Luftwaffe* adopted widespread rolling attacks starting with fighter sweeps over Kent at 0900 hrs, followed by another sweep at 1010 hrs. This second attack was probably the *Jabos* of II/LG 2 escorted by, amongst others, II/JG 54. As this plot was returning, another was appearing to the west of the Isle of Wight. This again was a *Freie Jagd* by Messerschmitt 109s and a few 110s which, whilst circling off the Needles, was bounced by 609 Squadron whose Spitfires were responsible for shooting down three Messerschmitt 109s; at the same time, *Hptm* Helmut Wick and *Oblt* Franz Fiby of *Stab* I/JG 2 were accounting for two 56 Squadron Hurricanes.

No real pattern to the attacks was evident until early in the afternoon when a much larger mixed formation was plotted heading for London. This was successfully intercepted and, although few German bombers were shot down, the remainder were turned back. What was thought to be the last attack in the east on that day occurred just before tea-time when a mixed formation of Ju 88s again headed for London together with a heavy escort of Messerschmitt 109s. The ensuing combats ranged from Kent almost into eastern Hampshire and saw many losses on both sides. For JG 26, it would be a particularly bad evening with their losing five fighters and four pilots, one of whom was just about to be given command of one of the *Gruppe* if the *Geschwader Kommodore* approved:

Hauptmann Walter Kienzle, *Stab*/JG 26

I was flying from Audembert with the *Stabschwarm* Maj Galland, *Oblt* Horten and one other whose name I cannot remember. We were supposed to be in formation with another fighter unit approaching southern England. From reports afterwards, I know that Galland attacked an RAF fighter and we were bounced – they must have got me. Galland told me afterwards that he saw my Messerschmitt fall like a fire ball and a parachute opened. I myself have no recollection of the event. I woke up two or three days later in a military hospital run by Canadians which specialised in pilots who had been shot down in flames. I was told that I landed almost in the hospital yard! As well as burns, my right leg had to be amputated just above the knee as it had been smashed when I baled out.

Hptm *Walter Kienzle*. (Kienzle)

Who shot Walter Kienzle down is not known for certain but one combat report comes close to the German pilot's recollections and the location where the remains of his fighter crashed:

Flight Lieutenant Gordon McGregor, 1 Squadron RCAF

...We sighted the bomber formation of about twenty-five with fighter escort above and behind of about forty Me 109s. About twelve dived down to attack. I held course through this attack and turned and engaged an Me 109 which was attacking a Hurricane. The Hurricane broke right and the Me 109 left where I opened fire. Towards the end of the full burst, he streamed smoke and spun down through clouds south of Brooklands.

The circumstances surrounding another German fighter lost in the same area at the same time were just as dramatic but, as it would later transpire, the unfortunate German pilot was a victim of friendly fire. A few years ago, the remains of a Messerschmitt 109 were discovered with evidence that the plane had been hit by 20mm cannon fire. No cannon-armed RAF aircraft were flying that day but one RAF pilot could have witnessed what happened:

Group Captain Stanley Vincent, RAF Northolt

...I climbed towards the sun and tried to attack an Me 109 but had to leave it owing to others coming down onto me from above but I saw three Me 109s chasing a Hurricane at right angles to me from left to right and when the Hurricane dived away (straightening out at 5,000ft below) and the Me 109s turned back on their course, I was able to get in a good position on the tail of the third one. Before I opened fire, I saw Number One burst into flames and the pilot jump out; he had obviously been shot down by the Number Two who was close astern of him...

Leutnant Herbert Schmidt, 6/JG 27

The last day of September 1940 – my last flight in the last war. Every year since that time I celebrate this day like a second birthday as it very much is.

In the afternoon, we had to protect bombers and got involved in heavy aerial combats with British fighters which caused our formation to break up. I remember that I pursued a Spitfire [sic]. It dived and I pulled back up for height. Looking around I was alone – a bad situation for a fighter. It was high time to fly back. Suddenly I saw tracer bullets exactly in my direction of flight and at the same time, my cockpit was full of flames. A terrible thought flashed through my brain – this is the end!

I tried to cast off the cockpit roof in order to get out. I lifted my left arm to do it but powerless, the arm fell down. I didn't know that it was smashed by bullets. I tried again and again and finally succeeded in getting rid of the roof. I couldn't see this but felt the fresh air penetrate the hell of flames and smoke I was sitting in. Now I tried to loosen the seat belts but couldn't manage it and lost consciousness.

When I recovered my senses, I was falling at high speed, turning somersaults. My first idea was open the parachute. It was very difficult to get the handle for my arm was following the turning movements of my body. With a great strain, I succeeded.

When the parachute opened, I thought I would be torn to pieces. Because of the high speed of the fall and the fact that nearly all of my clothing had been burnt away, so that the parachute harness did not sit close, the opening parachute caused a heavy blow to my body. Thereby my flying boots – plop! – fell away.

I floated in the air. Some things I still can see today. Three Spitfires roaming around and flying away. A look at the blackened tip of my nose and my black and bloody hands. No feeling of pain.

Suddenly a pain on my neck. Catching at it, I had a burning piece of my life jacket in my hand – my life jacket was still on fire. I tried to stub out the flames with my hands, always fearing that the parachute would catch fire and I would drop away like a stone.

Thank God it didn't happen. It took an eternity until I saw the ground. I made a safe landing near a road like a perfect parachutist, although I had never exercised this! I noticed two men standing by a truck. They came over to me. "Help!" I said and I heard one of them saying, "…badly burned…" Then blackout.

The following weeks were the worst of my life. I remember them like an awful dream. It is a wonder that I am alive but it would not be correct if I didn't mention the British and Canadian doctors and sisters who helped me when I thought I was at an end.

Lt Herbert Schmidt was flying this Bf 109 when he was shot down on 30 September 1940. (via Moelders)

As this German attack was disintegrating over the east, another was developing in the west when forty-three Heinkel 111s of KG 55 tried to attack the Westland Factory at Yeovil in Somerset whilst eleven Junkers 88s of KG 51 attacked Southampton. Yet again the formation, hampered by bad weather, was intercepted and turned back, the Heinkel 111s unknowingly dropping their bombs on the helpless town of Shaftesbury. The RAF fighters did lose six aircraft in combat with two being claimed by KG 51, eight by JG 2, two by JG 53 and, surprisingly, four by ZG 26. The latter unit suffered just one aircraft damaged but their success on this day did not influence the decision to continue withdrawing the Messerschmitt 110 from France. A further Messerschmitt 109 from II/JG 2 was lost in addition to four Heinkel 111s and a Junkers 88.

And so September 1940 finished – the *Luftwaffe* having lost thirty-one of its fighters in action that last day in addition to fourteen other aircraft. The RAF's debit sheet was just sixteen lost in action. It was an upbeat note on which Fighter Command could end the month. Despite its numerical superiority, the *Luftwaffe*, through the RAF's tenacity and German tactical errors and plain bad luck, had failed. It had almost achieved air superiority for the first six days of the month but with the change in tactics and emphasis, Fighter Command had won it back. Two aircraft types – the Junkers 87 and Messerschmitt 110 had been rendered impotent, the Dornier 17 was showing itself to be inadequate and the Heinkel 111 was starting to show its failings. These two aircraft would now be used more at night. The *Luftwaffe* hoped that the Junkers 88 would be the shining knight of its bombing fleets. However, without German air superiority, Fighter Command again and again broke up attacks by this aircraft type and inflicted heavy losses on the *Kampfgeschwader*. As to the effectiveness of the Messerschmitt 109 *Jabos*, they had so far been just an irritation to Fighter Command. But there was still one more month to go before the Battle of Britain was officially over – time for the Messerschmitt 109s, be they fighters or fighter-bombers, to try and regain air superiority.

4
The Final Chapter
– October 1940

The beginning of the new month was an anti-climax compared to the last day of the old one. The exact target of the aircraft that appeared off the Isle of Wight just before lunchtime was not clear but it appeared to fail in its objective, one of the escorting Messerschmitt 110s being shot down in the process. However, the Messerschmitt 109s of JG 2 were quick to punish the defending fighters, shooting down two each from 238 and 607 Squadrons and damaging another one from each Squadron; German claims matched exactly. Meanwhile, the first *Jabo* attack had already been launched against London, heavily escorted by various *Jagdgeschwader*. Only one single-engined fighter from each of the opponents was lost throughout the day.

A similar pattern followed the next day but on this occasion just heavily escorted *Jabo* attacks were carried out. This time, one of the new *Jabostaffeln* learned a valuable lesson:

Uffz *Kurt Buehligen of 4/JG 2 (seen here later during the war) shot down one of the Hurricanes off the Isle of Wight on 1 October 1940.* (Morzinek)

Gefreiter **Heinz Zag, 8/JG 53**

We were on our first *Jabo* mission on 2 October and our *Kette* was attacked from behind and three of us did not come home. Only my *Staffel Kapitaen* and myself were taken prisoner. The dogfight took place at 7,000–8,000m near London and my engine was hit and stopped – thank God it did not burn. I then glided down to land in a hop-field and during the crash-landing I was injured.

Oblt *Walter Radlick (far right) was the* Gr Adj *of III/JG 53 who was killed on 2 October 1940; he is seen here with other pilots from 2/JG 53. L to R:* Uffz *Hans Kornatz,* Lt *Rudi Schmidt (+ 15 September 1940),* Fw *Wilhelm Heidemeier (+ 11 July 1941),* Fw *Franz Kaiser (POW 21 April 1942),* Stfw *Ignatz Prestelle (+ 4 May 1942),* Oblt *Rolf Pingel (POW 4 July 1941),* Fw *Franz Gawlik,* Uffz *Josef Wurmheller (+22 June 1944), ?,* Lt *Walter Rupp (POW 17 October 1940).* (Rupp)

It was a bad start for III/JG 53 who not only lost three from 8/JG 53 including the *Staffel Kapitaen* but also the *Gruppen Adjutant*. 8/JG 53 was bounced by Spitfires of 603 Squadron who lost one Spitfire to a Messerschmitt 109 from 9/JG 53. The pilot who probably shot down Heinz Zag was luckier than that British pilot:

Sergeant George Bailey, 'A' Flight, 603 Squadron

After meeting enemy aircraft at 26,000ft, I lost height and saw enemy aircraft in cloud. After coming through the cloud, I saw AA fire and then sighted enemy again and opened fire at it from astern. He then began to lose height with a stream of glycol coming from the machine. I then followed it to about fifty feet when I lost sight of it…

With just one Spitfire lost throughout the day compared to the four Messerschmitt 109s, the RAF was the clear winner. However, the winner the next two days was the weather as the UK was blanketed in low cloud and drizzle. But on 5 October, apart from another bombing raid in the Portsmouth/Southampton area (JG 2 claiming thirteen when in fact only one British fighter was lost and a further two badly damaged), it was a series of rolling *Freie Jagd* and *Jabo* attacks to the east that concentrated the minds of Fighter Command's pilots.

28 October 1940: Oblt *Karl-Heinz Krahl,* St Kap *3/JG 2 (5th from right) and* Ofw *Rudolf Taeschner, 1/JG 2 (far right) claimed four Hurricanes between them on 5 October 1940; the reality was considerably less. Other pilots are, R to L Taeschner,* Oblt *Ulrich Adrian, I/JG 2,* Oblt *Hermann Reifferscheidt,* St Kap *1/JG 2,* Lt *Franz Fiby,* Adj *I/JG 2, Krahl,* Oblt *Rudi Pflanz,* TO *JG 2,* Oblt *Erich Leie,* Adj *JG 2 and* Reichsmarschall *Goering.*

As the Messerschmitt 110s from *Erprobungsgruppe* 210 took off from their base at Calais just before lunch, heading for Becton Gasworks and the airfield at West Malling, they were destined to meet an already alert Fighter Command that had been scrambled to counter a *Jabo* attack on London by II/LG 2:

Flying Officer Bobby Oxspring, 66 Squadron

The Squadron was vectored onto a hostile raid near Maidstone at 20,000ft. Half a dozen spasmodic AA shell bursts drew our attention to a *Staffel* of Me 109s flying south-eastwards from London. They were about our height as we initiated a streaming attack on them. The enemy were flying in loose pairs which broke formation as we closed into firing range. One yellow-nosed Me 109 broke left to right across my front and I got a nice three seconds burst on it from behind and beneath. He turned through the hazy sun as I repeated the dose which resulted in a stream of grey smoke.

The aircraft dived down and I followed, firing from close range. The rudder flew off and almost immediately the aircraft burst into flames. Our hurtling descent carried us uncomfortably close to a squadron of Hurricanes concentrating on a climb out. I had to giggle when our sudden spectacular arrival from aloft split the Hurricane formation which cascaded in all directions. In striving to avoid ramming one of my startled friends, I managed to glimpse the Me 109 spinning down near Lympne; there was no sign of a parachute...

Fw *Wilhelm Pankratz (sitting, 2nd from right) as a POW in Canada; other Bf 109 pilots are* Uffz *Andreas Wallburger, 2/JG 27, POW 15 September 1940 (front, far left),* Fw *Werner Gottschalk, 6/LG 2, POW 6 September 1940 (front, far right),* Uffz *Emil von Stein, 4/JG 2, POW 2 September 1940 (back, far left),* Uffz *Werner Karl, 1/JG 53, POW 2 September 1940 (back, 3rd from right) and* Uffz *Valentin Blasyewski, 6/LG 2, POW 14 September 1940 (back, far right).* (Karl)

The *Jabo* pilot was luckier than Bobby Oxspring thought – *Fw* Wilhelm Pankratz of 6/LG 2 did manage to crash-land and was taken prisoner. However, it was the 'startled' Hurricanes that were to cause the carnage that followed:

Unteroffizier Willi Ghesla, 1/JG 53

The night before this flight, I was on guard duty and so was not assigned to what would become my last flight. However, as the mission was only escorting Bf 110s as far as Dover (because of low cloud), I agreed to fly with my *Staffel*. Near Dover, the cloud was higher and our *Staffel Kapitaen* ordered us to fly on to London at 7,000–8,000m altitude. A comrade and I flew as cover for the rest of the *Staffel* just under the clouds. Suddenly, British fighters appeared out of the clouds and before being able to turn away, I received hits in the engine and oil cooler. I dived down to 4,000m, got my plane under control again and tried to make for Calais by gliding. But now I was fired at again and I lost consciousness for a short time. When I had a clear head again, I found myself near the ground and immediately looked for somewhere to land. I did not have a choice and I landed under difficult circumstances in a meadow. During this crash-landing (and because I had opened my seat belts instead of my parachute release), I hit my head on the *Revi* gunsight and got concussion. I quickly left my plane and walked to a

Uffz *Willi Ghesla*. (Ghesla)

nearby farmhouse where I was captured a few minutes later.

Pilots of 1/JG 53 just before 5 October 1940. L to R: Uffz Ludwig Reibel (+20 December 1942), Lt Alfred Zeis (POW 5 October 1940), Uffz Heinrich Ruehl (+ 4 June 1941), Hptm Hans Karl Mayer (+ 17 October 1940), Uffz Willi Ghesla (POW 5 October 1940), Oblt Hans Ohly, Lt Ernst-Albrecht Schulz. (Ohly)

It would appear that Willi Ghesla had been bounced by Hurricanes of 1 Squadron RCAF and it is possible that two Hurricane pilots from this Squadron were responsible for the two 1/JG 53 losses that day – Willi Ghesla and his *Rottenfuehrer, Lt* Alfred Zeis:

Flying Officer Hartland Molson, 1 Squadron RCAF

My recollection of 5 October 1940 is that on our way south from Northolt, we were jumped by some Me 109s. I believe that we were flying as a Wing with 303 (Polish) Squadron and 229 Squadron vectored onto a bomber raid coming over the coast towards Canterbury.

When I returned to altitude, as so often happened, everybody seemed to be a long way off and I was alone but a few miles ahead was a terrific dogfight in sight. Heading to join, I saw a pair of Me 109s well above the party cruising around looking for a victim and I was conceited enough to think that I might score on them. At full bore, I tried to get closer to the rear one, opened fire too far away; he half rolled out of sight and I thought perhaps I had damaged him. I tried to close on the leader of the pair. I neglected to keep my eye on the first one who, of course, simply came up behind me and shot me down.

As well as being the pilot that possibly shot down Willi Ghesla, this Canadian pilot was likely the victim of the following:

Leutnant Alfred Zeis, 1/JG 53

During our mission on 5 October, we were surprised by Hurricanes and some Spitfires. Due to the fighting, our formation broke up and we were forced to fight individually. In the course of these engagements, I shot at a Hurricane which was flying below me and attacking another Bf 109. However, I was then attacked from behind and was hit in the engine, radiator and the aileron controls. I tried, as best as possible with my severely damaged plane, to disengage and subsequently got further hits during different evasive actions. Finally, after a turn, the plane got in a spin and because of the battle damage, I could not regain control so I was forced to bale out; I never could have made it back to France.

It is now thought that Zeis lost control of his fighter because the hydraulics had allowed the undercarriage to drop down and therefore, in his attempts to get away, had caused him to lose control of the plane. Again, accounts of the combat on this day are vague but one Canadian pilot could have been the one that shot him down:

Flying Officer Paul Pitcher, 1 Squadron RCAF

My Pilot's Flying Log Book reveals the following entry in relation to the sortie in question (which, incidentally, appears to have been the first of three that day): "5 Oct 40 – Hurricane YO-D – (Duty) Patrol Base and Dover – Me 109s and 110s engaged – (Duration of Flight) 1.05 – 1 Me 109 destroyed – engaged and damaged one Me 110 – Port fuel tank hit."

There is no mention of the hour of day we scrambled on that sortie so I cannot tie in the time of the sortie with that of the crash of Lt Zeis's aircraft. As you can gather from the records, it was an extremely busy hour and five minutes and positive recollection of details is difficult. However, as far as I can recall, the 109s undercarriage dropped down and if this is what I reported to the Intelligence Officer on landing, this was my impression at the time.

My most vivid impression of the sortie was the landing back at base. My aircraft was not equipped with self-sealing fuel tanks and my port fuel tank had been riddled with bullet holes and the cockpit was awash with fuel. The air turbulence on landing caused clouds of fuel to swirl over the engine cowling and hot exhaust stacks and, by some miracle, the whole aircraft failed to explode.

Suffice it to say, the attack by *Erprobungsgruppe* 210 failed in its objective, with the loss of the acting *Gruppen Kommandeur* and three other crewmen and two more crew wounded. The escort fared no better with a total of six Messerschmitt 109s being lost during this and other attacks during the day; the RAF lost just two fighters in combat.

The scene was set to stay the same for many of the days that followed – poor weather, *Freie Jagd* and *Jabo* attacks. The only exception was 7 October which saw an improvement in the weather and the appearance, for the first time in a week, of escorted Junkers 88s targeting London and the Westland

Aircraft Factory at Yeovil. Mixed in with both formations were *Freie Jagd* and an audacious *Jabo* attack on London which cost the brother of the *Luftwaffe*'s top scoring fighter pilot his freedom:

Oberleutnant Victor Moelders, *Staffel Kapitaen* 2/JG 51

I joined JG 51 late in August 1940 as my brother wanted me to form a *Jabo Staffel*. I was given command of 2/JG 51.

Between 1000 hrs and 1030 hrs on the morning of Monday 7 October 1940, my brother tasked me to fly a mission. My *Staffel*, eight aircraft armed with 250kg bombs, were to take off from Pihen, climb to 6,000m, fly north to London and attack the Docks. We were then to fly back as quickly as possible. We were to be protected by the *Stab Schwarm* and eight aircraft.

As we approached the Thames Estuary, my brother informed me that he would remain at this altitude and return to Pihen as they were running low on fuel. I then dived with my *Staffel* and flew at rooftop height over the streets of London. It was funny to see the flak bursting above me! We dropped our bombs on the Docks and proceeded to return to France. Suddenly I heard the radio call "Indians behinds you!" and on looking saw about thirty aircraft at 6,000m diving towards us. I waited until they were close, then turned and flew towards them. All that I can remember after that is that I was hit in the radiator and I began to leak glycol and the engine temperature rose…

Maj *Werner Moelders (3rd from left)*,
Lt *Erich Meyer (POW
7 October 1940) and* Oblt *Victor
Moelders*. (Moelders)

The two Moelders brothers – Werner…

…and Victor. (Moelders)

Sergeant Eric Wright, 605 Squadron

Yellow Section was airborne at 0940 hrs and on patrol with 501 Squadron in the south London/Maidstone area. We sighted seven Me 109s flying east at 25,000ft and as we were 1,000ft above them, we dived down to attack.

Three Me 109s passed below me and I got in a two second burst at one from his stern quarter. He then dived and I gave chase and positioned myself underneath him where he couldn't see me. I got to 150 yards range then fired a seven second burst, seeing some smoke coming from the top of the engine cowling as he tried to climb away. I held my position and the smoke stopped. I then fired the rest of my ammunition at him and saw glycol coming from his wing radiator. I left him five miles south east of Maidstone, slowly losing height.

Oberleutnant Victor Moelders

...I decided to remain low as the engine was not capable of climbing. I got rid of the rear canopy and began switching the engine off and on. Looking behind I saw a lone RAF aircraft following me. I then went into cloud and when I emerged, I saw that this fighter was flying alongside me. He then broke away and I never saw him again.

The remains of Moelder's Bf 109E-4/B after its salvage. (via Payne)

I was too low to bale out so I began to look for a suitable field to land in. All the fields that I saw had old cars in them or other anti-glider obstacles. I eventually had to crash-land on top of an anti-tank ditch and did so too successfully – the aircraft showed no signs of burning. I tried to get out the flare pistol but couldn't and setting my map alight with my lighter and trying to start a fire also failed to destroy my aircraft.

Shortly after I was captured by some Home Guardsmen and put into a Rolls Royce and then taken for tea and cake in a house. Later I was taken to a police cell where I flushed my notes on the mission down the toilet and eventually handed my captors my pistol and other effects. The following day I was taken to London.

The results of these attacks were minimal – the damage at Westlands was slight and the Germans lost one bomber and, for the last time on a daylight mission over the UK, seven Messerschmitt 110s from II and III/ZG 26. The Messerschmitt 110s' last mission could have resulted in their total annihilation had the retreating formation not returned under the protection of the Messerschmitt 109s of JG 2.

As the month progressed, the weather worsened and the German bombers increasingly started to use the cover of darkness to achieve their aims. The RAF night fighter defence was very much in its infancy and it would be another month before they started to cause casualties amongst the *Kampfgeschwader*. Still, when the weather permitted, *Freie Jagd* and *Jabo* missions were flown but Fighter Command still had the upper hand. Casualties were still occurring on both sides but not on the same scale as the previous months. Fighter Command was still busy, now realising that it did have the superiority it wanted (as in fact it had for much of the Battle of Britain) and that *Jabo* attacks had to be countered. The final fighter actions of the Battle can best be illustrated by accounts from three different German pilots. The first relates to a combat on 12 October 1940:

Oberleutnant **Guenter Buesgen,** *Staffel Fuehrer* **1/JG 52**

I had flown about eighty missions with 1/JG 52 and had eight victories – all British. I had taken over command of the *Staffel* from *Oblt* Carl Lommel who had been posted away. I had been *Staffel Fuehrer* for three days when between 1500 hrs and 1530 hrs on 12 October 1940 I was shot down.

We had taken off from Calais in the afternoon on an escort mission. We accompanied bombers to London and as we turned for home the RAF fighters, as usual, attacked. It was a confusing battle but my *Rottenflieger* stayed with me. Suddenly, I looked behind and glimpsed what I thought was a fighter. I immediately dived – our usual tactic – and levelled out at 1,000m. The engine was vibrating – I had been hit. I climbed back to 4,000m and throttled back as the engine temperature was rising. I put the propeller into gliding pitch and turned for home. However, it was no good. The temperature gauge was reading hot so I jettisoned the rear part of the canopy and rolled her onto her back but nothing happened so I rolled back. As I did this, I fell out of the aircraft and was not prepared for it. As a result, I hit the fuselage and was injured.

I came down safely by parachute and was welcomed by the Home Guard. They removed my gun (and my pilot's badge and Iron Cross) and I was taken to a local hospital. Later I was transferred to a hospital at Woolwich.

Oblt *Guenter Buesgen on leave shortly before being shot down.* (Buesgen)

The victorious RAF pilot in this case is not known but is thought to have come from 92 Squadron. By way of contrast, the RAF was still suffering at the hands of the *Luftwaffe* as one inexperienced Spitfire pilot recalls:

Sergeant Clive Hilken, 74 Squadron

Flying from Biggin Hill in Spitfire Mark II serial P7426 as Number Three in Yellow Section of 74 (Tiger) Squadron on an interception at Angels 20, I had my first and short experience of a dogfight on the afternoon of Sunday 20 October 1940.

I decided when we broke formation to follow [Flt Lt] Mungo-Park, my Section Leader, whose Number Two had left us. I followed his straight climb, weaving behind him and keeping a wary eye on our tails. He was obviously gaining height in order to come down out of the sun. I found, of course, that by weaving I was dropping behind so I tried watching our tails without weaving and tried to keep up. After what seemed to be a few seconds, my instrument panel seemed to explode at the right hand side and explosions shook the aircraft. From the bottom of the cockpit, smoke came up and the aircraft was uncontrollable. I baled out at what must have been 20,000ft; my flying boots, however, remained in the cockpit. Also, I hadn't unhitched my oxygen tube and the rubber stretched and gave way without pulling my mask off, giving me what turned out to be a beautiful black eye to add to the many bits of cannon shell shrapnel which I received in my left hand, right arm, face and body.

When my 'chute opened, I was left swinging wildly at first in that very cold rarefied air and not a sign of aircraft anywhere near! I was most uncomfortable in my harness and tried to adjust the straps only to find I was gasping for breath at the least exertion.

Out of habit, I glanced at my watch and remember that it was 3.00pm. I landed over a quarter of an hour later through and down the side of a tree in an orchard. I was helped up by two Land Army girls and was pulling the 'chute clear of the trees after releasing the harness when a bit of 'Dad's Army' occurred! The farmer came round the corner of a hedge with his double-barrelled shotgun trained on me, ordering me to put my hands up. I soon convinced him that I was one of 'us' and he then proceeded to lead me limping in stockinged feet across his smelly fold-yard so that he could phone Biggin Hill and report my arrival and get some medical assistance.

Soon the Medical Officer came in the ambulance and took me back to Biggin Hill and on to Orpington Hospital to have a larger piece of shrapnel removed from my right upper arm and to have X-rays which revealed many more tiny fragments, many of which came to the surface in subsequent years.

I had landed near Tonbridge but my aircraft broke into parts and came down at Cowden, east of Westerham – the main part and cockpit in the woods of Leighton Manor and the other part (as I found out a few years ago by enquiring in the village) came down behind the 'Sun

Sgt Clive Hilken (far right) with Sgts Rex Mallet and Jamie Dyke (left to right). (May)

Inn' just as the family was finishing their Sunday dinner. It pierced the brick pond behind the pub and the pond leaked and never regained its original level! I knew that the cockpit had been found because my black flying boots had been returned to me – the finders had found them in the wrecked aircraft and returned them to the nearest RAF station which was Biggin Hill!

This was the first of three times that this young pilot was to be on the receiving end. The last time, 27 June 1941, he was taken prisoner of war. It is not known for sure who got the novice pilot but *Stfw* Helmut Goedert of I/LG 2 claimed a Spitfire at exactly the same time noted by Clive Hilken – 1500hrs.

The final two German accounts for October 1940 come from two pilots from two different *Geschwader* who were lost on the same day when, on the 25th, the German fighters and fighter-bombers returned in force to the skies over south eastern England:

Oberleutnant Jochen Schypek, 5/JG 54

The last pages of my logbook confirm that I took off at 1010 hrs Central European Time on 25 October 1940 and did not return from a mission escorting Bf 109s carrying 250kg bombs to London.

We were attacked when the bombers had reached London Docks and I yelled an alarm "Indians at six o'clock!" The warning was received and the bombers released their bombs and started a 180 degree turn. Seconds later, I had an 'Indian' in my rear view mirror and guessed it was a Spitfire. With them, we had developed a standard and often successful escape procedure – our Daimler Benz engines were fuel injection ones whilst the Spitfires had carburettor engines. That meant once we put our noses down vertically and quick enough, our engines would continue to function without interruption whilst the Spitfires – and Hurricanes – attempting to stick to our tails would slow down long enough for us to put a safer distance between them and ourselves. The slowing down was the consequence of the float in the carburettor getting stuck due to the sudden change in position.

I had managed to break away at least a dozen times by means of this manoeuvre but lo and behold, it did not work this time! The 'Indian' was right on my tail in my steep dive and opened fire. I could see bullets hitting my wings and, from the white trails on both sides, I knew he had hit my radiator. It all started at a rather high altitude – we had been approaching London at some 25,000–26,000ft and when hit I was still at more than 20,000ft. I throttled back as I knew it would soon seize. My 'Indian' drew alongside and the aircraft appeared strange to me as I had never been so close to a live Spitfire before. I was rather relieved that he recognised I did not have any chance of getting home and that he did not insist he completed his kill...

Lt *Jochen Schypek (right), August 1939.* (Schypek)

Flying Officer Peter Brown, 'A' Flight, 41 Squadron

I followed Red Leader and attacked an Me 109 – no apparent results. Having lost the Squadron, I climbed to 25,000ft again and saw about nine Me 109s on my starboard beam. I turned to attack them and was involved in a dogfight. After two short bursts, glycol poured from out of one of the Me 109s. I gave it two more bursts, slight deflection. The enemy aircraft rolled over on its side and dived straight into cloud.

I then attacked another Me 109 – followed it over the sea but after one burst, my ammunition ran out. First enemy aircraft is believed to have crashed in the vicinity of Rye. Two of my guns did not fire due to the cold.

Oberleutnant Jochen Schypek

...First human reaction, after trying in vain to report my fate to my *Staffel* Kapitaen so I knew that my radio must have been shot up too, was a series of curses followed by deliberations of what to do next. I had levelled out of my steep dive, saw my engine temperature was rising quickly and felt the first shuddering sensations in my aircraft – the signal that the seizing was already in progress. Stopping my curses, I remembered instructions to the point that it was possible to glide from south of London beyond the coast, ditch and wait to be picked up by one of our very courageous air-sea-rescue planes – provided you found the appropriate gliding angle and speed!

During the glide through the clear blue sky, other more personal thoughts occupied my mind. If I could not make it, I meant reach the Channel waters and be picked up, my engagement party would have to be called off (I had a fiancée in Vienna and the party was scheduled for Christmas if I could get leave). Could I get a message through to Roloff von Aspern (my *Staffel Kapitaen* and best friend) to go and pick up the engagement ring I had ordered at a jewellers in Lille? How long would it take to inform my widowed mother in Berlin that I was alive? Only then did I worry about the water temperature in the Channel – would I stay conscious long enough to experience my rescue?

Meanwhile, I was losing altitude at a terrifying rate and Dungeness, my point of orientation, came dangerously close. I was too low already to reach my desired destination and was about three miles from the coast and therefore missed the only opportunity of ever using my parachute. When I was low enough to see soldiers working behind the beach with shovels I made my decision to turn around and belly land.

I eventually touched the ground, rather gently I remember, skidded a little to the right. I had thrown away my cabin roof and had turned off the ignition long ago. Anyhow, I was in a hurry to get away from the plane for how could I know that it would not blow up?

I heard soldiers shouting and running towards me with threatening shovels! "Hands Up!" I put them up and could see a Captain approaching me at a quick pace. I do not recall when and how we agreed to speak English – he seemed quite glad that I knew the language. Together we took a closer look at my 'Black 7'. The rear of the fuselage was perforated with bullet holes – thank God that during the discussions following the French surrender that the

Jochen Schypek's 'Black 7'.

supporters of armour plating to protect the fuel tank and pilot won over those who did not wish to sacrifice an inch of altitude and speed – it certainly saved my life.

What followed was rather funny. The Captain pulled out a check list and registered my name and rank first and drew the automatic blanks when asking for unit, home base, etc. Next he wanted to have my pistol and was shocked that I only had my signal pistol to surrender. How could I enter enemy territory practically unarmed? I told him my 'arms' were in the aircraft wings and fuselage and in the narrow Messerschmitt cockpit a pistol holster was too much bother. I had to agree that by flying without a side arm, I had violated *Luftwaffe* regulations.

Next item: my map. When I said that I had none he was shocked again! A soldier in enemy territory without a map – how could I have ever dreamed of finding my way? I told him that the geography of southern England within the flying range of the Bf 109 was so easy to read that it did not require a map.

I was glad that I could co-operate when he wanted my parachute and life jacket. Meanwhile a vehicle, I think it was probably a weapons carrier, had pulled up and took me to Brigade HQ. I was introduced to a Colonel who rattled out some orders to the Captain which I did not catch. However, the result was I was turned over to a Lieutenant who marched me to the Officers' Mess.

I did have a watch but why I do not remember the hours when things occurred, I do not know. In a mess room I was served my first English tea – at home I never added milk – and some sandwiches. When it turned dark, I lay on a sofa and caught up on some sleep. Some noise at the door woke me up again. It was completely dark now with only an emergency light. In the darkness I recognised who had caused the noise and for seconds a terrific relief came over me – the person was my *Staffel* mate *Lt* Ernst Wagner. "Mensch, Ernst!" I cried. "Imagine what I had been dreaming just now: I was shot down and taken prisoner by the Tommies!" Ernst replied rather earnestly "That was no dream!" He had been caught during the second sortie of the day.

Gefr Karl Raisinger's 'Yellow 13'.
(via Cornwell)

There were many rolling attacks that day, Ernst Wagner crash-landing near Dungeness four and a half hours after Jochen Schypek. The experiences of another German pilot are very similar:

Gefreiter **Karl Raisinger, 3/JG 77**

On 25 October, we were flying to London – 1 and 2 *Staffeln* had bombs and 3 *Staffel* was escorting them. We were flying at about 10,000m and west on London, I saw many Spitfires and Hurricanes apparently waiting for us. Unfortunately, I had little experience as a fighter pilot and had to fly on the right flank of the formation (which was a fault) instead of the middle. When turning 180 degrees over London after the bombs were dropped, the British fighters attacked us and as I was without protection, they got me first.

I did not realise that I was hit. My plane was shaking but I thought because of the speed. But suddenly, there was smoke in my cockpit. I throttled back and tried to dive towards the Channel alone. To the south west I saw clouds and heard over the microphone that there was a lot of smoke coming from my plane. I disappeared into the clouds (I think it was raining) and came out and saw the coast. I was afraid to

The same 'Yellow 13' on display as an advertisement for National War Bonds. (via Cornwell)

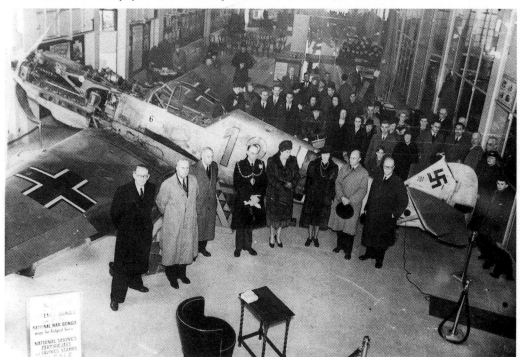

Karl Raisinger (centre) on his way to captivity. (via Raisinger)

force-land in the sea and as the propeller had stopped, I removed the cockpit roof. I was by now at 100m over the sea so I turned back and force-landed in a field near Brighton.

The cost on this day was eleven German fighters with three pilots killed and seven taken prisoner; the RAF lost in the region of ten fighters but only two pilots were killed. In the wreckage of one of the aircraft, the RAF thought that they had found evidence that one of their pilots had shot down an ace. The rudder of the Messerschmitt 109 that crashed near Marden in Kent showed forty-eight kills, the aircraft of JG 51's *Maj* Werner Moelders. However, Moelders was now flying the Messerschmitt 109 F (achieving his first kill on this type on 22 October and a further two on 25 October). *Hptm* Hans Asmus had been using his *Kommodore*'s old 'Emil' and it was he, not Moelders, who had been shot down and taken prisoner.

With autumn turning to winter, the weather allowed more twin engined bombers to use the poor conditions as a means of defence. But still, when the weather permitted, the fighters and fighter-bombers came. The last day of the Battle of Britain on which major fighter-against-fighter action occurred was 29 October and it is therefore fitting that the last account should come from one of the victorious RAF pilots. Fifteen Messerschmitt 109s were lost on this day, amongst whose pilots were three *Staffel Kapitaen* and two *Gruppen Adjutant*. RAF losses were just four fighters:

Flying Officer Tadeusz Kumiega, 17 Squadron

I do remember that sortie on 29 October although I admit I remember more vividly other encounters when I fired my guns in anger.

We took off from Martlesham Heath on what I think was the second sortie of the day. Though one is not aware at the time of the overall picture, I believe that we were scrambled to intercept the tail end of an offensive sweep by a token number of bombers and a strong cover of fighters and to cover returning squadrons as they refuelled. We spotted a formation of Me 109s at about 25,000ft and went into attack in then fashionable tight formation with the motto 'Follow my lead.' We were at once attacked from above and behind and a general combat resulted from it. Although eyes are primarily engaged in seeking a target in front of your guns and one's safety behind, I remember the criss-cross of tracers as shots were fired in this melee.

An Me 109, which later turned out to be the victim, crossed my path from port to starboard in a shallow dive some 1,000ft or more in front of me. I abandoned my rear view mirror, dived after him on full power and found myself directly behind him, his tail some 100ft or more from the barrels of my guns. I knew that I could not gain on him in my Hurricane so I opened fire.

One can sometimes see the bullets hitting the target. I could not – the tracers appeared some distance in front of the target but with a second, longer burst, I could sense the Me 109 twitch. He immediately turned on his back, dived and then pulled out. I lost the distance in that move but, as I put my aircraft in a tight turning dive, I saw another Hurricane pounce on the enemy and fire. By then we were much lower, some 15,000ft. Sgt Hogg overshot and I too managed only one burst before I had to pull up. The Me 109 lost power and was in a gliding descent, a faint smudge of coolant trailing him. He was directly underneath me and as I prepared to deliver another attack, the pilot waved his wings – to me a sign of surrender. Sgt Hogg joined me and, well throttled back, we followed him. But as he headed for the open sea, I gave him a short burst. He continued for a while, still heading for the sea and slightly waving the wings. I felt he might try to ditch out in the sea in the hope of rescue and I decided to terminate it. I do remember a moment of pure human sorrow for the enemy who lost but I delivered a burst from some 300ft and Sgt Hogg followed the lead. The Me 109 turned immediately on his back and a canopy of parachute bellowed up against the grey texture of the land below. We watched the aircraft dive vertically, hit the ground and explode in a plume of black smoke. Did I imagine it or did I see two horses galloping away across the field? It might have been then or it might have been from some dream or film from the past.

We returned to base immediately afterwards, reviewed the combat, wrote reports and agreed to the share. We later heard that the pilot of the Me 109 [*Ofw* Konrad Jaeckel of 8/JG 26] was in hospital following his landing on a parachute. I had the chance to see him but I declined. It was not until almost a year later that I added to my score: one undivided Me 109.

Epilogue

The *Luftwaffe* had failed. For just under four months, their fighters and bombers had tried to gain the air superiority they wanted so that the German Army could invade the United Kingdom. They could easily have achieved this, having essentially attained it in the week that preceded 7 September. But then they changed tactics and gave the overworked and numerically inferior RAF fighter pilots the breathing space they wanted.

However, for August and much of September 1940, in the words of the Duke of Wellington after the Battle of Waterloo, 'It was a close run thing.' Some say Fighter Command was lucky, others say the Germans were unlucky. However, it was the dedication of a small force of men, some of whom suffered and died for their cause, that stopped Hitler in his tracks and made him and his generals think again. Unknowingly, they changed the course of World War Two.

A hero's funeral – as the war progressed, many more German fighter pilots would be killed but not afforded such a magnificent ceremony. (Bezner)

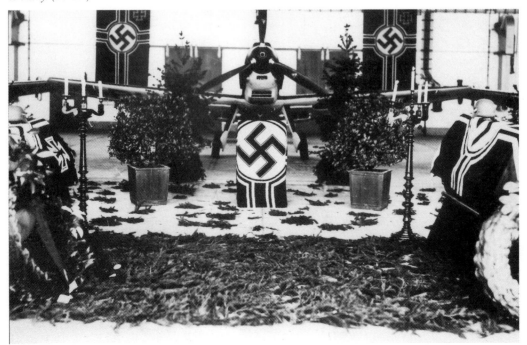

The period of the Battle of Britain is now celebrated from 10 July to 31 October 1940, with 'Battle of Britain Day' being 15 September. For the first time since 1940, today's RAF now celebrates it in the same way that the Royal Navy celebrates the Battle of Trafalgar. Nevertheless, it should be remembered that the first major *Luftwaffe* assault against the United Kingdom took place not during the Battle of Britain but on the night of 18/19 June 1940. Furthermore, following the official ending of the Battle of Britain on 31 October 1940, the months that followed saw no let up in the *Luftwaffe's* daylight tactics – in fact, for the first time since 18 August 1940, the *Stuka* appeared in the skies off the Kent Coast on 1 November, seeking shipping and losing one of their number. These daylight air battles were nowhere near as massive and furious and the night war now took precedence, forcing the RAF to develop and employ what would become a particularly effective weapon – the night fighter.

The German aircrew had suffered badly during the Battle of Britain and for many of those who had survived, they would either be killed or end up prisoners as many of their number had done during the summer/autumn of 1940. Likewise, many of the RAF fighter pilots would lose their lives. One such was Sgt John Glendinning. He had managed to shoot down five German aircraft before he too was shot down when, on 12 March 1941, it was his misfortune to become *Obstlt* Werner Moelder's sixty-first victim. By way of concluding this book on the German fighter pilot's Battle of Britain, John Glendinning's third kill on 15 November 1940 clearly shows that the 'Battle' was still being fought after its official close and would still be fought for another four and a half blood-stained years:

Sergeant John Glendinning, 'A' Flight 74 Squadron

I heard the shout "Snappers behind!" and broke away with my Section, weaving to the right and the left, and saw about twenty yellow-nosed Me 109s above me and on the port side. I immediately broke away to the right and turning steeply to both right and left saw four Me 109s going down in a vertical dive, attempting to catch a Spitfire. I tried to follow but could not get near. I again broke away and did climbing turns to 18,000ft. I was just levelling out when an Me 109 went past me on my port side. I delivered a beam attack and he

Sgt John Glendinning, killed in action 12 March 1941.

flipped over onto his back for a few seconds, seeming to hang in the air. I closed again and gave another burst, pieces flew in all directions and it went down in a series of rolls. Still not being satisfied, I gave it another burst and something seemed to explode inside the aircraft and the tail came away. I remember seeing the tail but the next I saw it seemed to be all pieces going into the sea four miles east of Bognor.

The man responsible for John Glendinning's death – Obstlt Werner Moelders. Glendinning is recorded as the sixty-first kill, fifth from the left on the bottom row of kill markings. (Moelders)

Gefreiter Rudi Miese, 4/JG 2

We took off from Le Havre. 4 *Staffel* had six aircraft under the leadership of *Lt* Meimberg and was at the rear of the *Geschwader* acting as *Holzaugestaffel*. I flew at the rear of the *Staffel* with *Uffz* Dessoy as my *Rottenfuehrer*. Shortly before reaching the English coast, we spotted coming from the left and below a formation of twelve to fifteen

Spitfires. Dessoy and myself swung to the left and attacked them from the front and above. The machine I attacked, I do not know whether I hit it or not as it rolled and dived away. We were already below the sun when we pulled back to the left when from above and the left and behind the cockpit, I was hit by tracer.

Immediately, the aircraft burst into flames and dived. Simultaneously, I threw off the cockpit roof and undid my straps. Then I lost consciousness and must have fallen out and the parachute opened. As consciousness returned, I was hanging about 1,000–2,000m up, swinging on the parachute quite violently, without flying boots and socks and a hole in my life jacket. I was still over the water but not far from the coastline. My hands and face were burnt and my left arm smashed. Two British aircraft circled me and the pilots waved to me.

I was blown by the wind nearer the coast and landed on a road by the beach without injuring myself further. About twenty civilians and a bobby came running. The policeman rolled up the parachute and pulled it away from me. Then an RAF doctor came – he gave me first aid and bandaged my arm in the street. I was then rushed by ambulance to a hospital in Littlehampton. Here they operated on my arm three times.

Gefr *Rudi Miese*. (Miese)

Lt *Julius Meimberg of 4/JG 2. He would survive the war having shot down fifty-six aircraft; he was shot down three times and badly wounded each time.* (Meimberg)

Uffz *Lorenz Dessoy of 4/JG 2. He was shot down and wounded at least twice during the war.* (Meimberg)

When I came round after the first operation in the evening after I was taken prisoner, by the side of my bed was an RAF officer who spoke good German and interrogated me. I did not answer him on questions about my unit but he reproached me for carrying my operational pilots pass, named my *Geschwader*, *Gruppe*, *Staffel* and the names of my *Kommodore*, *Kommandeur*, *Staffel Kapitaen* and all the pilots of 4/JG 2 as well as our airfield at Beaumont Le Roger and the operational airfields of Cherbourg and Le Havre. He also named the take off times from Le Havre (morning and afternoon) on the day I was shot down.

•

Dramatis Personae

	Date	Unit	Aircraft	Crew	Notes
1.	29 May 1940	1/ZG 76	Bf 110 D-1/R-1 M8+LL	*Oblt* Hans Jaeger (*F*) – POW; *Uffz* Helmut Feick (*BF*) – POW	Shot down by Hurricane of 46 Sqn and ditched off Salanger, Norway, 2000hrs
2.	1 June 1940	2/ZG 1	Bf 110 C	*Oblt* Juergen Moeller (*F*, *St Fhr*) – POW; *Uffz* Karl Schieferstein (*BF*) – POW	Collided in the morning with Spitfire off Dunkirk
3.	8 July 1940	3/LG 2	Bf 109 E-1 *Wk Nr* 2964	*Lt* Albert Striberny – POW	Shot down by Flt Lt B H Way, 54 Sqn and crashed at Buckland Farm, Sandwich, Kent 2000hrs
4.	11 July 1940	9/ZG 76	Bf 110 C-4 *Wk Nr* 3551 2N+EP	*Oblt* Gerhard Kadow (*St Kap*, *F*) – POW; *Gefr* Helmut Scholz (*BF*) – POW	Shot down by Sqn Ldr J S Dewar, 87 Sqn and Fg Off H K Riddle, 601 Sqn. Crash-landed Povington Heath, Lulworth, Dorset, 1210hrs
5.	28 July 1940	Stab/JG 51	Bf 109 E-3	*Maj* Werner Moelders (*Gesch Komm*) – W	Damaged in combat with Flt Lt J T Webster, 41 Sqn and crash-landed at Ste Inglevert, 1540hrs
6.	11 August 1940	1/ZG 2	Bf 110 C	*Lt* Wolf Muenchmeyer (*F*) – uninj; *Uffz* Fritz Labusch (*BF*) – uninj	Damaged in combat off Portland and crash-landed at Theville
7.	11 August 1940	1/ZG 26	Bf 110 D	*Hptm* Hans Kogler (*St Kap*, *F*) – W; *Uffz* Adolf Bauer (*BF*) – W	Damaged in combat off Harwich and ditched, 1310hrs; crew rescued 14 August 1940
8.	12 August 1940	Stab III/JG 54	Bf 109 E-4	*Oblt* Albrecht Dress (*TO*) – POW	Probably shot down by Flt Lt M N Crossley, 32 Sqn; <–+ crash-landed Henmore, Margate, Kent, 1800hrs
9.	13 August 1940	1/ZG 2	Bf 110 C-4 *Wk Nr* 3201 3M+LH	*Lt* Wolf Muenchmeyer (*F*) – POW; *Uffz* Fritz Labusch (*BF*) – +	Shot down by Sgt L Guy, 601 Sqn and crashed at Knightwood Farm, Flexford, Hants 1600hrs
10.	15 August 1940	1/ZG 76	Bf 110 D-1/R-1 *Wk Nr* 3155 M8+CH	*Oblt* Hans-Ulrich Kettling (*F*) – POW; *Ogefr* Fritz Volk (*BF*) – POW	Shot down by Plt Off E A Shipman and Plt Off G H Bennions, 41 Sqn, and crash-landed at Streatlam near Barnard Castle, Co Durham, 1335hrs

No.	Date	Unit	Aircraft	Crew	Notes
11.	15 August 1940	6/ZG 76	Bf 110 C M8+BP	*Fw* Jakob Birndorfer (*F*) – + *Uffz* Max Guschewski (*BF*) – POW	Shot down by Plt Off J Zurakowski, 234 Sqn and Plt Off P Ostazewski-Ostoja, 609 Sqn, and crash-landed at Ashey Down, Brading, Isle of Wight, 1806hrs
12.	16 August 1940	*Stab* III/ZG 76	Bf 110 C	*Lt* Richard Marchfelder (*TO, F*) – POW *Ogefr* Herbert Jentzsch (*BF*) – POW	Possibly damaged by 602 Sqn; crew baled out and aircraft crashed at Droke Cottages, East Dean, West Sussex, 1830hrs
13.	18 August 1940	6/JG 2	Bf 109 E-4	*Oblt* Rudolf Moellerfriedrich – POW	Shot down by Flt Lt P C Hughes, 234 Sqn and crashed at Tapnall Farm, Brookdown, Isle of Wight, 1440hrs
14.	24 August 1940	1/JG 52	Bf 109 E-1 White 9	*Fw* Herbert Bischoff – POW	Shot down by Flt Lt D G Gribble, 54 Sqn and crash-landed Minster Road, Westgate on Sea, Kent, 1545hrs
(15.)	25 August 1940	1/JG 53	Bf 109 E-1 White 15	*Gefr* Josef Broeker – POW	Shot down by Plt Off R P Beamont, 87 Sqn, Plt Off W Beaumont, 152 Sqn and Sgt R T Llewellyn, 213 Sqn; crash-landed Tatton House Farm, Buckland Ripers, Dorset, 1730hrs
(16.)	25 August 1940	1/ZG 2	Bf 110 C-4 Wk Nr 3208 3M+KH	*Uffz* Siegfried Becker (*F*) – POW *Uffz* Walter Woetzel (*BF*) – POW	Shot down by Plt Off N le C Agazarian and Plt Off G N Gaunt, 609 Sqn, and crashed at Priory Farm, East Holme, Dorset, 1800hrs
17.	26 August 1940	2/JG 2	Bf 109 E-4 Wk Nr 5383	*Oblt* Hans-Theodor Grisebach (*St Flhr*) – POW	Shot down by Plt Off A E A Van den Hove-d'Ertsenrijk, 43 Sqn and crashed at Newbarn Farm, Blendworth, Hants, 1725hrs
18.	28 August 1940	7/JG 51	Bf 109 E-4 Wk Nr 1523 White 14	*Ofw* Artur Dau – POW	Probably shot down by Sqn Ldr P W Townsend, 85 Sqn and crashed at Garden Wood, Poulton Farm, Houtham, Folkestone, Kent, 1655hrs

No. & Date	Unit	Aircraft	Crew	Circumstances
19. 30 August 1940	4/ZG 76	Bf 110 C, Wk Nr 3615, M8+MM	Ofw Georg Anthony (F) – +, Uffz Heinrich Nordmeier (BF) – POW	Shot down by Fg Off B J Wicks, 56 Sqn and Fg Off L W Paskiewicz, 303 Sqn; crashed at Barley Beans Off Farm, Kimpton, Herts, 1630hrs
20. 31 August 1940	8/ZG 26	Bf 110 D, Wk Nr 3396, 3U+HS	Oblt Erich Von Bergen (F) – POW, Uffz Hans Becker (BF) – POW	Shot down by 257 Sqn; crashed into sea between Colne Point and East Mersea off Essex Coast, 0830hrs
21. 31 August 1940	14(Z)/LG 1	Bf 110, Wk Nr 3617	Lt Karl-Joachim Eichhorn (F) – POW, Uffz Richard Growe (BF) – +	Shot down by Fg Off H T Gilbert, 601 Sqn and ditched off Foreness Point, 0905hrs
22. 31 August 1940	14(Z)/LG 1	Bf 110, Wk Nr 3805, L1+AK	Fw Gottlob Fritz (F) – POW, Ogefr Karl Doepfer (BF) – POW	Shot down by Fg Off C R Davis, 601 Sqn and ditched off Nore Light, Thames Estuary, 0910hrs
23. 1 September 1940	5/JG 54	Bf 109 E-4, Wk Nr 1277, Black 14	Oblt Anton Stangl (St Kap) – POW	Collided with another Bf 109 and crashed at Capel Farm, Bonnington, Ashford, Kent, 1115hrs
24. 1 September 1940	7/JG 26	Bf 109 E-1, Wk Nr 3892, White 11+I	Lt Josef Buerschgens (St Fhr) – POW	Shot down in error by Bf 110 and crashed at Newbridge Iden, Rye, East Sussex, 1403hrs
25. 2 September 1940	1/JG 53	Bf 109 E-4, Wk Nr 3584, White 14	Uffz Werner Karl – POW	Shot down by Fg Off A G Trueman, 253 Sqn and Sgt J H Lacey, 501 Sqn; crash-landed Hythe Ranges, 0817hrs
26. 2 September 1940	1/JG 51	Bf 109 E-1, Wk Nr 4850	Lt Helmut Thoerl – POW	Shot down by Sqn Ldr J A Leathart, 54 Sqn and crashed at Abbey Farm, South Poston, Kent at 0830hrs
27. 4 September 1940	8/ZG 76	Bf 110 C-4, Wk Nr 3101, 2N+CN	Oblt Hans Muenich (F) – POW, Uffz Adolf Kaeser (BF) – POW	Shot down by Plt Off P W Horton and Sgt Z Klein, 234 Sqn; crash-landed Black Patch Hill, Patching, West Sussex, 1345hrs
28. 5 September 1940	9/JG 53	Bf 109 E-1, Wk Nr 6252	Fw Anton Ochsenkuehn – POW	Shot down by Plt Off J Zurakowski, 234 Sqn and ditched south of Hastings, 1538hrs

No.	Date	Unit	Aircraft	Crew	Details
29.	6 September 1940	*Stab* I/JG 2	Bf 109 E-4 *Wk Nr* 5044	*Lt* Max Himmelheber (*Adj*) – POW	Possibly shot down by 601 Sqn; crashed Plumtree Farm, Headcorn, Kent, 0900hrs
30.	8 September 1940	*Stab* I/JG 53	Bf 109 E-1 *Wk Nr* 3478	*Oblt* Heinz Wittmeyer (*Gr Adj*)– Inj	Collided with Bf 109 E-7, *Wk Nr* 1171 flown by *Oblt* Heinz Kunert, *St Kap* 8/JG 53 and crashed off Cap Gris-Nez
31.	9 September 1940	5/JG 27	Bf 109 E-1 *Wk Nr* 3488 Black 13	*Oblt* Erwin Daig – POW	Damaged in combat and crash-landed at Chitty's Farm, Cootham, East Sussex, 1822hrs
32.	9 September 1940	1/JG 53	Bf 109 E-4 *Wk Nr* 1508 White 5	*Fw* Heinrich Hoehnisch – POW	Probably shot down by Flt Lt W G Clouston, 19 Sqn and crashed at Cherry Lodge Farm, Old Jail Lane, Biggin Hill, Kent, 1800hrs
33.	15 September 1940	1/JG 53	Bf 109 E-4 *Wk Nr* 5194 << +	*Fw* Herbert Tzschoppe – POW	Shot down by Plt Off A D J Lovell, 41 Sqn and crashed at Adisham Court, Canterbury, 1210hrs
34.	15 September 1940	2/LG 2	Bf 109 E-7 *Wk Nr* 2058 Red 2	*Uffz* August Klik – POW	Shot down by Fg Off L A Haines 19 Sqn and crash-landed at Shellness Point, Isle of Sheppey, 1450hrs
35.	18 September 1940	*Stab* II/JG 53	Bf 109 E-1 *Wk Nr* 4842 White 10	*Lt* Erich Bodendiek (*TO*) – POW	Shot down by Plt Off R W Oxspring, 66 Sqn and crashed at Guilton Ash, Sandwich, Kent, 1705hrs
36.	27 September 1940	*Stab*/ZG 76	Bf 110 D-3 *Wk Nr* 4215 M8+XE	*Oblt* Wilfried von Eichborn (*Adj, F*) – POW / *Uffz* Erich Bartmuss (*BF*) – +	Probably shot down by Plt Off P A Worrall and Sgt G C Palliser, 249 Sqn and ditched off Hastings, 1000hrs
37.	30 September 1940	*Stab*/JG 26	Bf 109 E-4 *Wk Nr* 5818	*Hptm* Walter Kienzle – POW	Possibly shot down by Flt Lt G R McGregor, 1 Sqn (RCAF) and crashed at Roundhurst, Haslemere, Surrey, 1705hrs
38.	30 September 1940	6/JG 27	Bf 109 E-1 *Wk Nr* 3859 Yellow 3	*Lt* Herbert Schmidt – POW	Believed shot down in error by another Bf 109, and crashed at Holman's Grove, Grayswood, Surrey, 1640hrs

No.	Date	Unit	Aircraft	Pilot	Circumstances
39.	2 October 1940	8/JG 53	Bf 109 E-1 *Wk Nr* 6370 Black 3+1	*Gefr* Heinz Zag – POW	Probably shot down by Sgt G J Bailey, 603 Sqn and crash-landed at Forge Farm, Goudhurst, Kent, 1000hrs
40.	5 October 1940	1/JG 53	Bf 109 E-4 *Wk Nr* 1804 White 10	*Uffz* Willi Ghesla – POW	Probably shot down by Fg Off H de M Molson, 1 Sqn RCAF and crash-landed in between Frith Farm, Aldington and New Barn Farm, Bilsingdon, Kent, 1145hrs
41.	5 October 1940	1/JG 53	Bf 109 E-4 *Wk Nr* 1564 White 3	*Lt* Alfred Zeis – POW	Possibly shot down by Fg Off P B Pitcher, 1 Sqn RCAF and crashed at Sheerlands Farm, Pluckley, Kent, 1140hrs
42.	7 October 1940	2/JG 51	Bf 109 E-4/B *Wk Nr* 4103 Black 1	*Oblt* Victor Moelders (*St Kap*) – POW	Probably shot down by Sgt E W Wright, 605 Sqn and crash-landed on Lidham Marshes, Doleham Farm, Guestling, East Sussex, 1115hrs
43.	12 October 1940	1/JG 52	Bf 109 E-3 *Wk Nr* 1966 White 11	*Oblt* Guenter Buesgen (*St Fhr*) – POW	Probably shot down by 92 Sqn and crashed at Bean's Hill, Harrietsham, Kent, 1530hrs
44.	20 October 1940	74 Sqn	Spitfire II P7426	Sgt C G Hilken – wounded	Possibly shot down by *Stfw* Helmut Goedlert, 1/LG 2; aircraft broke up in between Cowden and Leighton Manor, Kent, 1500hrs
45.	25 October 1940	5/JG 54	Bf 109 E-4 *Wk Nr* 1988 Black 7	*Oblt* Jochen Schypek – POW	Shot down by Fg Off M P Brown, 41 Sqn and crash-landed at Broom Hill, Lydd, Kent, 0930hrs
46.	25 October 1940	3/JG 77	Bf 109 E-4 *Wk Nr* 5104 Yellow 13	*Gefr* Karl Raisinger – POW	Damaged in combat and crash-landed at Harvey's Cross, Telscombe, Saltdean, Sussex, 1330hrs
47.	15 November 1940	4/JG 2	Bf 109 E-4 *Wk Nr* 5949 White 10	*Gefr* Rudi Miese – POW	Shot down by Sgt J N Glendinning, 74 Sqn and disintegrated off Felpham, West Sussex, 1615hrs

Select Bibliography

Caldwell, Donald, *The JG 26 War Diary, Volume 1, 1939-42*, Grub Street, London, 1996

Caldwell, Donald, *The JG 26 War Diary Volume 2, 1943-45*, Grub Street, London, 1998

Collier, Richard, *Eagle Day*, Pan Books, London, 1968

Eimannsberger, Ludwig Von, *Zerstoerergruppe*, Schiffer Military History, Atglen, 1998

Everson, Don, *The Reluctant Messerschmitt*, Portcullis Press, Redhill, 1978

Foreman, John, *Fighter Command War Diary, Part 1*, Air Research Publications, Walton on Thames, 1996

Foreman, John, *Fighter Command War Diary, Part 2*, Air Research Publications, Walton on Thames, 1998

Goss, Christopher, *Brothers in Arms*, Crécy Books, Bristol, 1994

Mason, Francis, *Battle over Britain*, McWhirter Twins, London, 1969

Obermaier, Ernst, *Die Ritterkreuztrager der Luftwaffe, Band 1*, Verlag Dieter Hoffmann, Mainz, 1989

Oxspring, Gp Capt Bobby, *Spitfire Command*, Grafton Books, London, 1987

Payne, Michael, *Messerschmitt Bf 109 Into the Battle*, Air Research Publications, Walton on Thames, 1987

Price, Dr Alfred, *Battle of Britain Day, 15 September 1940*, The RAF Air Power Review, Volume 2 No 2

Prien, Jochen, *Chronik Des JG 53 Pik As, Band 1*, Flugzeug Publikation, Illertissen

Prien, Jochen & Stemmler, Gerhard, *Messerschmitt Bf 109 im Einsatz bei Stab und I/JG 3*

Prien, Jochen & Stemmler, Gerhard, *Messerschmitt Bf 109 im Einsatz bei II/JG 3*

Prien, Jochen & Stemmler, Gerhard, *Messerschmitt Bf 109 im Einsatz bei III/JG 3*

Prien, Jochen, Rodeike, Peter & Stemmler, Gerhard, *Messerschmitt Bf 109 im Einsatz bei Stab und I/JG 27*

Prien, Jochen, Rodeike, Peter & Stemmler, Gerhard, *Messerschmitt Bf 109 im Einsatz bei II/JG 27*

Prien, Jochen, Rodeike, Peter & Stemmler, Gerhard, *Messerschmitt Bf 109 im Einsatz bei III/JG 27*

Ramsey, Winston (Ed.), *The Battle of Britain Then and Now, Mark III*, Battle of Britain Prints, London, 1985

Sarkar, Dilip, *Through Peril to the Stars*, Ramrod Publications, Malvern, 1993

Sarkar, Dilip, *Bader's Duxford Fighters*, Ramrod Publications, Worcester, 1997

Vasco, John, *Bombsights over England*, JAC Publications, Norwich, 1990

Vasco, John & Cornwell, Peter, *Zerstoerer*, JAC Publications, Norwich, 1995

Wynn, Kenneth, *Men of the Battle of Britain*, Gliddon Books, Norwich, 1989

Index